TAKE
YOUR
PLACE

YOU SEE A LOST CAUSE...
I SEE A TURNAROUND

TAMSIN EVANS

RIVER
PUBLISHING

River Publishing & Media Ltd
Barham Court
Teston
Maidstone
Kent
ME18 5BZ
United Kingdom

info@river-publishing.co.uk

Scripture quotations taken from:
NIV - Holy Bible, New International Version®, NIV® Copyright © 1973, 1978, 1984, 2011 by Biblica, Inc.® Used by permission. All rights reserved worldwide.

NLT - Holy Bible. New Living Translation copyright© 1996, 2004, 2007, 2013 by Tyndale House Foundation. Used by permission of Tyndale House Publishers Inc., Carol Stream, Illinois 60188. All rights reserved.

MSG - Copyright © 1993, 1994, 1995, 1996, 2000, 2001, 2002 by Eugene H. Peterson.

ESV - The Holy Bible, English Standard Version Copyright © 2001 by Crossway Bibles, a division of Good News Publishers.

NAS - Copyright © 1960, 1962, 1963, 1968, 1971, 1972, 1973, 1975, 1977, 1995 by The Lockman Foundation

ISBN 978-1-908393-46-3

Details of some names and places have been changed to protect people's identities. Where possible, the author has verified stories with those involved. Each story is told to the best of the author's recollection.

Project editor Christina Boonstra
Illustrations by Rebecca Tamaklo www.rebeccatamaklo.com
Author photograph by Nathan Johnson
Cover design by www.spiffingcovers.com
Printed in the United Kingdom

CONTENTS

Section 3 – THE CHALLENGE OF FLYING

ACKNOWLEDGEMENTS

Tina, thank you for your belief in this message and your obedience to God. You will never know the huge encouragement you have been and I am blown away by your sacrificial sowing into the editing, critiquing and weaving together of this book. Huw Williams, thanks for your support of Tina through this.

Nick, thank you for bearing the cost of me writing this, for praying with me and for me. For listening to the chapters and caring deeply about this message. For staying up until 3am with me the day I submitted the manuscript. Thank you for pushing me into adventure, pushing me into God, for challenging me to be the best version of myself. You are the most incredible husband a girl could ask for. I love you. Joshua and Lois, thank you for being such a joy. It is an honour to be your Mummy. I really hope you know how immeasurably precious you are to us as you grow up as adventurers, who will each "Take your Place" as your lives unfold.

Mum and Dad, thank you for believing in me, loving me so well and creating an atmosphere for me to grow up knowing God and pursuing His plans for me. Matt, you are the best brother I could ask for. Thanks for our awesome chats. I really respect and value you.

Kirsten and John, thank you for believing in me and supporting me to do the work of Pure. I really appreciate you.

To all who have believed in me and cheered me on through the years, really too many to name... Joy Martin, Bel Reynolds, Nic and Jen Harding, Mark Harland, Kerry Connolly... Damian Wharton, for all your encouragement and support through the past 16 years. Lou, for being there through the highs and lows of this process. I am so grateful. Becci, for the beautiful birds and making the vision a reality! Jonnie and Liz, for taking the reigns of this new season of Pure UK – I could not have asked for better. Tim, thank you for believing in this book. Your support has meant a lot.

Most importantly, above anyone else: God, thank you for making it so clear I was to do this and showing me each step of the way. This is yours and for your glory.

PREFACE

For a long time I wrestled with whether I had heard God accurately about the call on my life. Was it really to reach young people in the Western world? I struggled with how much we generally have in Western society and reasoned that surely it would be better for me to go to an under-developed country far away. Why would God call me to people who seem to have so much compared to the rest of the world? I was so moved as I read about the homeless children in Mozambique in Heidi Baker's book *There is Always Enough* that I recommitted my life to God and cried out for Him to send me wherever He wanted me to go. But as I sought Him, His reply was this:

"Tamsin, I have called you to the starving, it's just a different kind of starving. I have called you to the starving in the Western world – to the desperate, the hopeless, to those starving themselves to reach an impossible image, to the eyes empty of dreams and without passion or vision."

Recently, I had a conversation with someone who works for Compassion, a charity that works through local churches around the world to release children from poverty to fulfil their God-given potential. On a recent visit to some of the projects they ran, she met some of the children they were working with and was struck by their incredible dreams and aspirations. One boy in particular lived in a faraway, remote village, which you could only get to by walking. There was no doctor in this village and if someone was sick, they had to walk miles and miles to get help. This boy, who was supported by Compassion, had told her in detail about his dream to be a doctor. He'd researched it and even knew exactly what type of doctor he wanted to be. Why? Because he could see the very real need in his village and through Compassion's investment he believed that God could help him make a real difference.

Compare this to the thousands of young people we've met through the work of Pure and you hear a different story. This year we've taken our production *The Other Side* into schools across the UK. At the end of the performance teachers can choose which workshop they'd like us to run with the pupils. There are three options, but in almost every school they choose the one about hopes and dreams. Why? Teachers tell us it's because this is what so many pupils are desperately lacking. Many of their pupils have no real hopes, no aspirations. As a result they turn to crime or harmful relationships. They struggle with depression, anxiety and much more.

This need may be harder to see at first, but actually poverty is a very real problem in the West. In England alone 13 million people, of which 3.5 million are children, are living in poverty. Having recently been funded by the Church Urban Fund, I know that they recognise that poverty is not just about income and, to illustrate this, they categorise poverty in three areas: the poverty of resource, the poverty of relationship and the poverty of identity

In one of my journals I noted down a dream I had:

"I dreamed last night that I was in a classroom, and we had been given the task to share our dreams, but nobody got up, because no one had any. As I stood up I was crying, because I had so many dreams, and within these dreams was the dream for each of these others to dream..."

Through the work of Pure Creative Arts, little by little, I believe we're seeing this change. When we've asked pupils what they've learnt at the end of these workshops about hopes and dreams they've responded with answers like, "That anything is possible ... talk to people if you need help ... don't get pressured into trouble ... never give up." But this is just the very beginning.

It is time for people in the West to wake up from their sleep and take their place.

We have an enemy and though it seems his strategy has been far more subtle in the West than in other parts of the world, it has silenced a generation. Simon Guillebaud, a missionary who works in Burundi, says this in his book *Dangerously Alive*:

"We face the same enemy in the West, although he is much more subtle in his attempts to lead us astray. Indeed, materialism, relativism, spiritual apathy and general busyness seem far more effective weapons than such blatant attacks. "

There is a far greater battle at stake here than I think many of us are aware of. This book is a call: a call to wake up, a call to surrender and a call to join an army that God is raising up. An army alive with the dreams that God has given them and ready to bring hope to a generation which is so desperately seeking it. There is a need to do this now, more than ever. If we don't wake up and step up to take our place in this battle, what will become of our nations?

To answer this call means hard work. It will be costly, painful, heart breaking at times and it doesn't pay well, but I believe there are thousands upon thousands that God wants to use. Through this book I use my own story, my own struggles and vulnerability to illustrate the challenges for each us stepping up to this call. I have used personal stories to be more engaging in the hope that it will shed greater light on what this practically might look like for you. I don't want this book to be about me, but about you and an invitation to step out further into the incredible journey God has for your life.

Are you willing to take your place in what He has for you? If so, the call is for you regardless of your age. God wants to speak to you and call you into adventure with Him like never before.

This book is dedicated to the generation of young people rising up from our schools with revival stirring in their veins. The ones who don't know it yet and the ones who have heard and are still to take their place – the promise of a generation. It is time!

Tamsin Evans
November 2014

1

TURNAROUND

You see an earthquake, I see an opening
You see a car wreck, I see you hope again
You see a dead end, I see you breaking through
You seem worn out; I'm making all things new

You see lost cause, I see a turnaround,
You see unwanted, I see you finally found
You see a locked cage, I see an open door.
You see dry bones; I see fire in your soul.

(Lyrics by Christina Boonstra, Tamsin Evans and Rael James)

Becky ran to the bathroom. Loud sobs followed. I looked to where she had been sitting and saw several large pools of blood on the sofa. Then on the floor, more blood than I had ever seen. My heart dropped. Becky was three months pregnant at the time and it looked like she was having a miscarriage right here in our home. Five minutes earlier I had been talking about how God can turn impossible situations around. We were praying with our team of leaders for the impossible to happen through a youth project we were running. Now, right in the middle of it, this had happened?

I ran to the bathroom and found Becky crouching on the floor, surrounded by a growing pool of blood. There was no way the baby could still be alive. Holding her sobbing frame I began to say, "I'm sorry, I'm so sorry." Then I stopped myself. What was I saying? Did I believe what I had been saying just five minutes earlier? Did I believe God could turn this around? I began to pray, speaking life to the baby inside Becky. I commanded a turnaround in Jesus' name, a reversal of what I could physically see. Faith began to rise up in me. I stopped worrying about whether my prayers of faith would hurt Becky if she lost the baby. Instead I put my focus on God and what He could do in this situation.

In the hall, Greg called Becky's husband Dave while someone else called an ambulance. The paramedics brought in a wheelchair to take Becky, still heavily bleeding, to the ambulance. In shock we stood at the door as the blue lights flashed down the street and out of sight. Closing the door left us to face the pools of blood that were still on the floor and the only thing we could do was pray.

"God, don't let it end like this, a cold room, pools of blood on the floor. We believe you for a turnaround. Let the baby live."

Later that night I received a text message from Becky. The doctors had told her that she had miscarried and they would do a scan to confirm tomorrow. Then, a little later they examined her and discovered her womb was still closed. How could it be? It didn't make any sense. The next afternoon she had a scan and, to their amazement, the doctor found a heartbeat. The baby was alive! Becky was never given a medical explanation for what happened – that night we saw a miracle.

Eight months later, as I held Becky's healthy baby girl, Mia, in my arms, I felt God whisper to me:

"When the blood is on the floor, when it looks like it is all over, dead and gone, this is where I begin. I am the one who turns it around, who resurrects, who brings life from dead things. Believe."

Every day we hear stories of incredible need and excruciating pain. A boy who is bullied commits suicide. A woman is gang raped, mutilated and left for dead. A teenager takes drugs for the first time and dies that night from a heart attack. These are not made up stories. These things have happened to sons, daughters, sisters, brothers…

We live in a world where the unthinkable happens every day and, in the midst of such chaos and pain, the flame of hope flickers out and gets lost so easily. Yet I know that even in the darkest, most impossible situation, God can do more than we can fathom, hope for, or imagine. But so often we struggle to believe it.

Perhaps our logical minds have pushed the possibility of the miraculous out of the way. Maybe we've prayed for a miracle and have been disappointed when things didn't turn out as we had hoped or based what God can do on our past experiences. There are many reasons why we don't pray like God can really change things. It hurts too much, it's too scary, we don't want to look stupid. But when we do this we are placing trust in ourselves and we are not allowing our trust to rest in mighty God. He is the God who turns situations around, not us. Our faith and trust has to be in Him. All, in Him.

In the Old Testament, there is a prophet called Ezekiel who God uses to call the Israelites, who have lost hope, back to Him. In a vision, God shows Ezekiel a valley full of dry, dead bones and asks him if he thinks these bones can live again. Ezekiel replies, "Lord, only you know."

"The Lord took hold of me, and I was carried away by the Spirit of the Lord to a valley filled with bones. He led me all around among the bones that covered the valley floor. They were scattered everywhere across the ground and were completely dried out. Then he asked me, 'Son of man, can these bones become living people again?'" (Ezekiel 37:1-3 NLT)

Then God commands Ezekiel to speak to the dry bones and

command them to come back to life. As Ezekiel obeys what God has said, he has to push against his fear and what he can literally see and instead believe in something bigger than himself; to speak out and command life to come into what is dry and dead. As he obeys, he sees the impossible happen:

"So I spoke the message as He commanded me, and breath came into their bodies. They all came to life and stood up on their feet—a great army." (Ezekiel 37:10 NLT)

God gives this vision to Ezekiel because He wants the Israelites to know that even though they had lost hope and felt like they were just dry, dead bones, God is able to turn the situation around. He is able to form an army out of dry bones.

I believe that is us. Though we're weak, broken, maybe even hopeless, God wants to breathe life into dry bones and raise up a new army. But not an army like the world knows it. Instead, an army of men and women who are fuelled by love and positioned to speak life into hopeless situations; who stand up for the broken and help those who are hurting. He is calling us out of our comfort zones to fulfil the plans and purposes in our lands that He has created us for.

So often we sit back and just let things happen. We don't like to think we are in a battle or that we have a part to play. John Piper writes,

"Most people show by their priorities and casual approaches to spiritual things that they believe they are in peace, not in wartime ... in wartime we are on the alert. We are armed. We are vigilant ... Probably the number one reason why prayer malfunctions in the hands of believers is that we try to turn a wartime walkie talkie into a domestic intercom. Until you know that life is war, you cannot know what prayer is for ... But what have millions of Christians done? We have stopped believing that we are in a war. No urgency, no watching, no vigilance. No strategic planning. Just easy peace and prosperity. And what did we do with the walkie talkie? We tried to rig it up as an intercom in our houses – not to call in fire power for conflict with a mortal enemy, but to ask for more comforts in the den..."

There's a phrase in the book of Joel, which always gets me when I read it:

"Thousands upon thousands are waiting in the valley of decision." (Joel 3:14 NLT)

I always picture the thousands who are waiting. Waiting for someone to come and tell them that there is another side to what they see. Waiting for someone to come and show them a worthy reason for making that decision.

Take Amy, for example. I met her when she ran out the hall during a production that Pure Creative Arts were doing in her school. Her teacher and I found her sobbing uncontrollably in a corridor. The performance she had been watching was about a girl who was raped and I could see that it had triggered something very painful in her. I began to chat with her, ask her what was wrong, but she wouldn't tell me. She just sobbed and shook her head saying, "It can't change anything."

Those words chilled me. I began to tell her stories of what I had seen God do in the lives of other people who had experienced rape. Stories that would give her faith and hope for her own future and help her to believe that God could do this in her situation.

Eventually Amy told me what had happened to her. As she did, it was like a weight literally lifted off her. I told her about God, who created the universe, who loves her, created her and made her for a purpose. I talked about the cross and how we can lay our pain, shame and hurt there. I prayed with her and her friends.

I believe that those who are in the valley of decision need us to have faith for them, to rise up ourselves beyond that which we know or can physically see and have faith in God for their impossible situations.

Where they see a lost cause, we need to show them what God sees – a turnaround.

If you ever travel to Vietnam you'll find that the roads are like nothing you've experienced before. There are no road signs, no crossings. Whole families pile onto one scooter. Even small children with no helmets hang off the scooters as their parents weave through the busy traffic. When you want to cross the road, you just have to step out and trust the traffic will weave its way around you. And generally it does.

When I visited, to begin with I was terrified, but after a while I got used to it and, in the midst of this chaos, God spoke to me. In the West we have become very risk averse, but God doesn't call us to a risk-free life. He asks us to step out and take a risk with Him. To take a step without having the whole route marked out. He asks us to obey Him, one step at a time, putting our full trust and confidence in Him alone.

Choosing to see the turnaround in the face of a lost cause is risky – it takes faith and courage – but this is what we were made for.

When we give our lives to God, He shows us the truth about who He created us to be. As we allow Him to work in us and through us, His power lives in us and is able to transform the circumstances and situations all around us. God wants to work through us to bring His hope. We each have a unique part to play in our lifetime. There is a call to step up and partner with the God who is limitless.

Will you take your place?

Section 1
IDENTITY

Before a bird can fly,
it must discover what
it was made to be

2

WEEDS

Among childish games a weed can spring up.
A little lie is planted and silently
it begins to dig deep roots down into a young heart.
In the dark it grows and grows, stretching up into the mind,
taking hold of anything in reach,
Until there is nowhere in that mind
where its shadow is not cast.

My arm was covered in green slime. What was it? Kate and I had been playing a game in my room when her skirt got caught, and I noticed that she wasn't wearing any knickers. Then I noticed there was this bright green slime on the floor where she had been sitting. To my disgust, some had got on my arm. Feeling sick, I ran to the bathroom to scrub it off. Something about the bright green colour of the slime concerned me. Uncertain of what to do, I quickly gave Kate a pair of knickers to put on. Why didn't she have knickers on? Surely that wasn't normal. My mum would never let me go out without underwear. Was Kate okay?

I avoided her after that day. I was embarrassed and confused about the discovery I had made. I couldn't make sense of what had happened, yet for some reason felt so ashamed that I didn't speak to anyone about it, not even Kate. Instead, I spent time with other friends, choosing to ignore her until she slowly slipped out of my mind and disappeared.

A few years later, around the time we started secondary school, my best friend Erica saw a poster with a picture of Kate on it. In large letters underneath the image it said: MISSING.

When Erica told me what she had seen, something tightened around my heart, quaking emotion through my body. Was it shame? Embarrassment? Where did it come from?

"Remember that girl, Kate? You were friends with her, right? They said she ran away."

I shrugged off the news, pretending I didn't care, but underneath my heart was racing.

Was it my fault that she ran away? Was it because I had ignored her? After that day at my house I had known Kate wasn't okay, but instead of saying something to someone, I kept quiet. Instead of being her friend, I ignored her because I was ashamed. This shame grew like a weed inside of me. It wrapped itself around my secret, taking root in my heart and stretching up into my mind.

I grew older... but the weeds remained.

A few years later I was squashed in the back of a car on my way for the first time to a large Christian conference called Spring Harvest. Music blared out from my walkman as we drove down the motorway to Skegness, stopping off at a rather unglamorous Little Chef. As we drew nearer, the traffic slowed to a crawl and we joined the deluge of cars with bumper stickers declaring, "We're going to Spring Harvest"!

This weekend away way was different to any holiday I'd been on before. And it wasn't the Butlins holiday venue that made it special. Or even how grown up my friends and I felt in our own chalet with our own key. There was expectancy in the air as people gathered from all over the country to meet with God. As we piled into our venue, filled with the scent of sweet, sweaty grime, I was struck by the passion of the people who were leading our youth meetings. They were so full of excitement for Jesus; I wanted to be like them. We had come to meet with God and He was here. I loved the worship, the talks and the presence of God. I wanted to soak it all in, to learn more, and grow in understanding.

At the end of the first night, a lady standing at the front of the meeting began talking about how there was nothing you could do that would stop God from loving you. Suddenly the weed I had forgotten about tightened its grip around my heart. Doubt clouded my mind as I was reminded of the shame I had felt all those years ago. I had a secret that I could not share. God couldn't love me, I thought, what I had done was unforgivable.

I vowed that the only person I would ever tell this secret to would be my husband. But only after we were married, so that once he found out he couldn't leave me. And that was that. My secret was locked up and the weeds grew faster around my heart. At the end of each meeting one of the leaders at the front would ask if anybody wanted to be prayed for, and each time I desperately wanted to go forward. I wanted to experience this love that they talked of with such passion. But the shame I felt held me stuck to the spot. I still didn't believe that God could forgive what I had done.

* * *

When the weed of shame has room to grow, it will set up house around a fragile heart. Stifling creepers wrap you into silence and whisper that your secret is safe in this house of weeds. If ever this lie is challenged, the weeds tighten their grip. A cold coil of memory shoots through your mind and chills you back into your silent prison.

* * *

The second evening meeting had, once again, captivated me, but then when they asked if anybody wanted to be prayed for, shame left me chilled.

After it ended my friends and I were out looking for adventure and made our way to Crazy Jack's, an afterhours venue open especially for youth, where a band called The Tribe was playing. There was something about this band that was different to anything I had ever seen before. It wasn't the dancing, or even the music, though I loved both. It was their unmistakable passion for Jesus. They wanted to make Him known. They wanted to see Jesus impact their city, their nation. They were passionate, radical, a little crazy, and I was hooked.

We stayed until the very end and they finished that Good Friday evening with a song about the cross. As I watched them sing, the words knocked the breath out of me:

"When will you see? That He died for you?" (The Cross, World Wide Message Tribe)

This truth cut straight through the weeds that had wrapped themselves around my heart for the last six years. And in that moment I realised that the cross was not some far off gruesome tale. Suddenly I saw it was real. It was for me and it made all the difference.

"But the fact is, it was our pains he carried—our disfigurements, all the things wrong with us. We thought he brought it on himself, that God was punishing him for his own failures. But it was our sins that did that to him, that ripped and tore and crushed him—our sins! He took the punishment and that made us whole. Through his bruises we get healed. We're all like sheep who've wandered off and gotten lost. We've all done our own thing, gone our own way. And God has piled all our sins, everything we've done wrong, on him, on him." (Isaiah 53:5-6 MSG)

What Jesus had done was enough to pay for my sin. To overcome those weeds of shame that that had locked up my heart and kept me hiding. On the cross He took the punishment that I deserved, so I could be free. The least I could do was accept it and finally see that He had died for me.

How many times had I replayed that day in my mind, adding up my mistakes and concluding that I could not be forgiven? How many times had I tried to quantify what the almighty God could forgive and what He could not forgive? When had I decided that my weak childlike mess would be too much for Him?

How had I let this thought grow into a huge weedy garden that separated me from Him?

I stood there, tears streaming down my face, overwhelmed by the truth that had finally torn down those old weeds around my heart. That truth was stronger than any lie I had believed about what I had done. Stronger than the vow of silence I had taken. Something radically changed that night. I felt lighter, finally free. Before me was a fresh start, a blank sheet of paper, and the question beckoned: what was I going to do with it?

3

GETTING REAL

Shame is a lie that can lock up our hearts. It tells us that we can't share our pain with others; that the people we trust the most will judge us if we show them our failings; treat us differently, decide who we are.

Each one of us has been offered the gift of a fresh start at the cross. That clean slate is open to anyone who is willing to receive it. Yet time and time again, I've seen that weed of shame keep people locked up just like I was, preventing them from receiving the forgiveness that Jesus bought us.

"He cancelled the record of the charges against us and took it away by nailing it to the cross." (Colossians 2:14 NLT)

Fast forward a few years and I was speaking on the topic of purity at an event. Near the end of the meeting I felt that God wanted to meet with people who were locked up by shame, specifically those who had suffered abuse in the past.

As the meeting came to a close, one of the team called me over. She had been praying with a girl about being free from a sense of shame, but nothing was happening. It was like there was something in the way and she was at a loss as to what to do next. I suggested that we pray and asked the Holy Spirit to show us what to do. As we prayed I felt the Holy Spirit say, "Forgiveness" and I shared this with her:

"Have you been able to forgive the person who did this to you?" She shook her head. She told us that she had been given counselling in the past, but she had not been able to forgive. However, it wasn't the other person she was struggling to forgive, it was herself. We spent some time with her, talking about the cross and the power of forgiveness, then took her through a simple prayer of forgiveness to pray when she felt she was ready.

The more we talked the more we realised how much this sense of shame was holding her back from God. The shame was so strong that she couldn't bring herself to tell us what had happened to her. In that moment I was reminded of how freeing it can be to bring hidden things out in the open. Secrets wrapped in shame lose their power when they're brought into the light. I began to tell her about how ashamed I felt as a child after what happened with Kate. How I had vowed I would never tell anyone until I got married. How I had only ever told my husband. Even telling her then, in front of one of the members of my team, was tough. But I felt that the Holy Spirit was prompting me and that my vulnerability in this moment was important.

When I finished telling her my story, she asked if she could tell us what had happened to her. As she brought her secret out into the light we watched as God pulled the weeds away. Afterwards we prayed for her and a member of our team saw a picture of a heavy cloak being taken off her. At the same time she told us that she felt a loving hand on her head, even though no one had touched her head. The shame had lifted and suddenly she felt light and free.

Vulnerability is something we need to be careful with, and it's not appropriate with everyone. But sometimes, with people we trust, it leads to freedom. In our culture we've rejected vulnerability. Perhaps it's because we are bombarded with airbrushed images that make us feel like we need to reach some impossible ideal. Perfectionism is worshipped by the culture around us. Maybe that's why we don't like to show our shortcomings. Even in churches, it is so easy to begin thinking that the people on the stage are flawless. So often we only see their best side and start thinking that we need to be "perfect" like them. But no one is perfect. Perfection is impossible and we need to learn to embrace the vulnerability of our weakness and not reject it.

"Our rejection of vulnerability often stems from our associating it with dark emotions like fear, shame, grief, sadness and disappointment – emotions that we don't want to discuss, even when they profoundly affect the way we live, love, work and even lead. What most of us fail to understand, and what took me a decade of research to learn, is that vulnerability is also the cradle of the emotions and experiences that we crave. We want deeper and more meaningful spiritual lives. Vulnerability is the birthplace of love, belonging, joy, courage and creativity. It is the source of hope, empathy, accountability and authenticity. If we want greater clarity in our purpose or deeper or more meaningful spiritual lives, vulnerability is the path." (Daring Greatly, Brene Brown)

Do we know the real impact that locking up our secrets has? When we hide away our vulnerability, we fail to embrace who we really are.

Being vulnerable is a key part of knowing our God-given identity and moving forward into what we were made for. When we are set free from the weeds that have caught our hearts, we are brought into a spacious place to see and dream God's dreams again.

"He brought me out into a spacious place; He rescued me because he delighted in me." (Psalm 18:19 NIV)

And the question beckons for each one of us, once we have this space, what will we do with it?

4

SET APART

A treasure hunt begins with a clue. Every clue leads to another. With patience and perseverance, trial and error we move one step closer to the treasure hidden within.

The first clue

I awoke with anticipation the morning after my encounter with the cross. The lightness I felt as I walked back to my chalet after Crazy Jacks closed had remained. Those weeds of shame really had gone and now it was as though there was all this space before me, full of possibility.

Like a treasure hunt awaiting me, the very first clue about what God had made me for was about to be presented, but would I realise it?

There was a new freedom as I spent time in the meetings that day. In our worship times, we sang this phrase 'I could sing of your love forever' over and over. I had such a sense of peace and love from God. I really did want to sing of His love forever.

After our evening meeting we found ourselves at Crazy Jack's again. That night, a YFC theatre team called Activate was set to perform. The main reason we had decided to go was that our small group leader for the week, John, was part of Activate, and I think we all had a small crush on him. I don't remember much of what happened in the performance, but as I watched them something within me whispered, "Tamsin, you're going to do that. I want you to join Activate." It was like a match had been struck, lighting up darkness for a few seconds before it flickered away. Could God speak to me like that? I wasn't sure. It wasn't something I had experienced before and almost immediately I brushed it aside. The very idea of joining Activate thrilled me to the core and therefore, I reasoned, it couldn't be God. God only called people to faraway places! Like my youth leader Michelle who went to Brazil. Why would He tell me to do something I actually enjoyed, like join a performing arts team?

Looking back, I don't think it was a coincidence that I heard God speak to me for the first time the night after I finally discovered I could be forgiven. It was as though the forgiveness I had received had cleared the way, leaving a space for me to hear God speak.

Even though I sincerely doubted that God had spoken to me, the thought stuck. The next day I picked up a form about joining the Activate team at the YFC stand, which I kept safe in a box at home. In reality I was 13 and joining Activate was not even a possibility for another five years.

A seed had been planted, the first clue to the treasure trail had been given, but there was still a long way to go.

The second clue

Spring Harvest ended and before I knew it, I was fully immersed in friendships and studies again after the Easter Break. It was the summer term before we started year 10 and it was time to choose which subjects we would be studying next year. Like most people, I always wanted to know what I was best at. I would look at my friends and measure myself against them, trying to find the thing that I excelled at. It always frustrated me that my two closest friends usually achieved slightly higher grades than I did. What was I best at? One day I expressed this frustration to my Mum and she shared the Bible with me in a way that I've always remembered: "If you delight yourself in the Lord, Tamsin, He will give you the desires of your heart. What are the desires of your heart, Tamsin? What do you love?"

"Delight yourself in the Lord, and He will give you the desires of your heart." (Psalm 37:4 ESV)

This idea that God could give us the desires of our hearts, along with the whisper that I would join the Activate team in the future, was hard for me to get my head around at first. Somewhere along the line I had developed this idea that following God's plan for my life would mean doing something I didn't want to do.

Perhaps it's because the only people I had encountered who were "following God's call" were missionaries. A few people from my church had been sent out to war torn nations or countries in extreme poverty. Another one of my youth leaders had spent some time working with drug gangs in Hong Kong alongside Jackie Pullinger. All of this really scared me. It had never occurred to me that God would ask me to do something I actually enjoyed.

It's easy to take this verse out of context until we've twisted it around to mean that God will give us whatever we want. But that's not what this verse is saying. It's saying that as we get to know God, worship Him, enjoy Him and learn to love His presence more than anything else, our heart becomes aligned to His and His desires become our desires.

God has made each of us completely different. You are like no one else. He made the unique pattern on our tongues, our fingerprints and the retinas of our eyes. He designed our personalities, our likes and dislikes. And when we come to know who He is, we discover more of ourselves. God didn't make us to be clones of Him or each other, He made each of us unique with a unique mark to make on the world.

It frustrates me that we live in a world where uniqueness is not really celebrated. Through school, through magazines, through fashion and popular culture there is a status quo that we can so easily get caught up with. Sure, some of us choose to rebel from this and form other groups or types, but often these groups just serve as a different type of status quo.

What would it take for us to just be ourselves, to really be true to who we are?

"For we are God's masterpiece. He has created us anew in Christ Jesus, so we can do the good things He planned for us long ago." (Ephesians 2:10 NLT)

Growing up, I am not sure I saw myself as God's masterpiece. I often wished I was blonde like my friend Becky, or popular like Erica. I spent a lot of time comparing myself to others, wishing I was more like someone else than like me. That way of thinking became normal, habitual even. I didn't know that God viewed me as a masterpiece, just as I am, and if someone had told me that I don't think I would have believed them.

Still, my Mum continued to remind me that God could use what I loved doing. I loved drama and music and chose to study these subjects further as I started my GCSEs. In drama lessons I flourished, grew in confidence and excelled. Here was the second clue.

The third clue

The encounter I had with the cross at 13 stayed with me and the way God spoke to me was locked in my heart. At home I was privileged to go to a church where we had great youth leaders who would pray for us, spend time with us and lead us in the presence of God. Every week we would meet to worship God, and then in smaller groups they prayed for us to be filled with the Holy Spirit. For me nothing dramatic happened, but I believe

God was working in my heart dropping little seeds of dreams that would later flourish. I came to love being in God's presence and spending time with Him.

Reconciling this time with my experiences at school wasn't easy. After Tuesday night in youth group I would go home on a high from experiencing God's presence. The next morning as I walked into school this feeling stayed, but school was so different. There were no other Christians in my year and my friends were facing all kinds of challenges.

There was my friend, Lelia, who I sat next to in English. Lelia had an eating disorder. Her arms were covered in thick dark hairs because she wasn't eating enough to regulate her body temperature. She looked drawn and tired. How could I help her? I had experienced God's love and the power of the cross and I knew God could make all the difference in Lelia's situation. But I didn't know how to help her connect what she was going through with this God who I had come to know so well. When I tried to explain, my words seemed hollow; they were not enough to pierce the reality she lived in. Surely there was more that could be done?

At times I took my best friend to church with me. I wanted her to experience the Holy Spirit and the God I knew. For her, the experience provoked lots of questions. She felt a sense of peace, but couldn't see how this could affect her life.

Then there was our friend Chloe, who had been attacked by a group of girls in our year for sleeping with a guy that another girl liked. Someone held Chloe's head down while the others kicked her face until she was bloody and bruised. I was so scared after that and secretly glad that I had not been there when it happened. But the question hovered over me: what would I have done if I was there? Would I have been able to stop it or would I have run away? What difference could God make in this situation?

Another close friend was being sexually abused by her uncle and at the same time becoming sexually active with her first boyfriend. We talked and talked about how she didn't have to sleep with her boyfriend, but she didn't want to listen to me. How could God come into this situation and help her? I knew He could, but I knew more was needed to help her overcome the struggles she was facing.

It went on and on ... self-harm, depression, suicide attempts, drugs ... I watched with surprise as my friend tried drugs for the first time while on a school trip to see *Romeo and Juliet* in Manchester. Her eyes were wild like a cat. She almost jumped out of her skin when our teacher, Mr Sanderson, spoke to her. He looked at her as if he knew, but did nothing about it. For her it was a fun experiment; what being a teenager was all about. I knew there was more than this, but how could I show her?

Even though I knew God, and desperately wanted to see His power break into each situation, I couldn't see how. I felt weak and inadequate. Slowly, I stopped speaking about my faith. I became quiet and shy, nervous of what people thought of me, worried about what they'd say.

I was silenced.

"A word out of your mouth may seem of no account, but it can accomplish nearly anything – or destroy it! It only takes a spark, remember, to set off a forest fire. A careless or wrongly placed word out of your mouth can do that. By our speech we can ruin the world, turn harmony to chaos, throw mud on a reputation, send the whole world up in smoke and go up in smoke with it, smoke right from the pit of hell." (James 3:5-10 MSG)

The Bible says that the tongue has the power of life and death. Like this passage from James says, with our tongues we can cut people down or we can build people up. We can encourage or we can criticise. I don't think it's much of a surprise that our tongues are one of the three parts of our body to have a unique print. We all have a unique mark to make with the words that come from our tongues.

I stopped speaking about my faith because my friends were always talking badly about people behind their backs. I didn't want to join in with them, but if I told them what I was really thinking, what would they say about me behind my back? Instead, I became the quiet one.

In those years frustration grew. But frustration is not always a bad thing. Frustration, as a wise man once said to me, is seeing where you want to be but not being able to get there yet. The pieces of the puzzle were coming together, but I couldn't see it yet. I didn't get this perspective or recognise the clues or the treasure until quite a bit later.

5

THE HALL OF MIRRORS

"Come on Tamsin, we are going to be late!" This was the cry often heard in my house throughout my secondary school years.

School was a minefield of inadequacy. Each morning I would get ready, put my makeup on, and think I looked okay. But somewhere on the journey between home and school, something mysterious happened. When I arrived at school, the mirrors in the toilets always reflected the image of a girl who was not pretty enough and not good enough. And I wasn't the only one who felt this way. It seemed all my friends were struggling with the same issue.

Lunch and break times were spent in the toilets, sitting by the mirrors as my friends and I applied and reapplied makeup. The only exit from this toilet prison was if you started to date someone. So I was left to face the mirrors.

"Has anyone by fussing before the mirror ever gotten taller by so much as an inch? If fussing can't even do that, why fuss at all? Walk into the fields and look at the wildflowers. They don't fuss with their appearance – but have you ever seen colour and design quite like it? The ten best-dressed men and women in the country look shabby alongside them. If God gives such attention to the wildflowers, most of them never even seen, don't you think He'll attend to you, take pride in you, do His best for you?" (Luke 12:25-28 MSG)

Without realising it, the environment I was in had started to rub off on me. Just like almost all of the other girls in my school, I spent far too much time worrying about my appearance in the hope that I'd get the attention I was looking for. But I was looking in entirely the wrong place.

Guys rarely paid any attention to me. I was quiet at school and most of the time I felt almost invisible. When they did pay any attention to me, it wasn't the kind I wanted. I still remember the words that were spoken by some boys in my physics class one day:

"I'd shag you with a bag over your head. You have a fit body, but I can't be doing with your face."

"You'll never get a ring on your wedding finger. Who is going to marry you?"

Words have power and these words stuck stubbornly to me. I began to think my face was not pretty enough and layered on more makeup every day. Maybe they were right? Fear knotted in my stomach. Maybe no guy would ever want to marry me?

Slowly these lies began to affect my thinking. I started to believe that unless someone wanted to date me, I was not worthwhile. And without even realising it, weeds began to grow around my heart again.

"And I want women to get in there with the men in humility before God, not primping before a mirror or chasing the latest fashions but doing something beautiful for God and becoming beautiful doing it." (1 Timothy 2:9-10 MSG)

I had bought into the lie that my appearance was what mattered, rather than what I did for God. My focus was beginning to rest on the way I looked, not the condition of my heart.

I loved God, I read my Bible and still attended church and youth group. I did very much want to do something beautiful for God, but I didn't see how this worked at school. I couldn't understand how to fit these two lives together and felt I had failed doing that so far.

When a Christian Union started at my school, I really wanted to go, but sometimes I was too scared to leave my friends in case they talked about me behind my back. I desperately wanted their approval and that need was shaping decisions I made.

When I was 15, I went to a Christian festival called Soul Survivor with my youth group for the first time. In that week, a lot of things changed, but those changes were built on poor foundations.

Soul Survivor was wonderful. There was such a sense of the presence of God in each meeting and space for the Holy Spirit to work in our lives. More than anything, I loved the time to really pursue God in worship and the prayer times.

But there were also other things that made this time away significant. The first was Rachel. Rachel and I were part of the same youth group, but we had never really been friends before. She thought I was boring and girly and I thought she was a tomboy with greasy hair. At Soul Survivor we found ourselves together, however, and once we started chatting we couldn't stop. We soon became inseparable as we connected over our passion for God, our desire to live our lives for Him, and also over two very good looking brothers we had just met!

Late one night, as I left a group of my friends to find my tent, Will, the older of the two brothers, pulled me towards him for a kiss. I kissed him quickly and then ran away. For the first time ever here was a guy who was interested in me and even though I had always wanted to honour God in my relationships and never just date anyone for sake of it, I adored having this attention.

Here's where things got mixed up. For the rest of that week at Soul Survivor, my mind was on meeting with God, yes, but it was also on this guy, Will. In meetings, as I worshipped God, I became distracted by the possibility of what could happen between Will and me. Even though nothing did end up happening, these ideas replayed in my mind and took my attention away from God.

Maybe without this distraction God could have used this time to heal the hurt caused by those negative words at school. Maybe He would have shown me that none of it mattered – that He could be the one I looked to for affirmation. Instead, I thought this attention from Will might be the answer to my problems, and to be honest, it felt like it was working.

But the root of the problem had not been solved. My old fears were still there. They were just being covered up with this new feeling of being wanted.

After that summer, it seemed like everything changed. For the first time in a while, I was happy. With the new friends I'd grown close to at Soul Survivor, my life outside of school came alive. I was suddenly popular, suddenly wanted. But deep down, I was still searching for answers to the same questions. Was I pretty enough? Good enough? Clever enough?

Now that I had found approval from this new group of friends, my confidence grew. But all of it was built on a shaky foundation. My self-worth was still based on what other people thought of me, instead of what God thought of me.

"And then what happened? Well, when Israel tried to be right with God on her own, pursuing her own self-interest, she didn't succeed. The chosen ones of God were those who let God pursue His interest in them, and as a result received His stamp of legitimacy. The 'self-interest Israel' became thick-skinned toward God. Moses and Isaiah both commented on this: Fed up with their quarrelsome, self-centered ways, God blurred their eyes and dulled their ears, shut them in on themselves in a hall

of mirrors, and they're there to this day." (Romans 11:7-9 MSG)

My constant desire to impress left me consumed with my own reflection. Desperate to evoke the right reaction from others, their opinion of me had become more important than what God thought. It had become my idol. We can never build our lives on the opinions of others. If we do this, we'll use up all our strength working to impress, and though it may work for a while, eventually we will come to realise that it's never enough.

I was shut in a hall of mirrors, doing life my own way, and talking to God as I went along.

How God must have longed to tell me how *He* saw me. But I was too busy chasing after something else. A habit had formed. Even though I loved God, I was more focused on meeting my own needs than obeying Him. Ultimately that was sin and I was setting myself up for a fall.

6

HEART

"Guard your heart above all else, for it determines the course of your life." (Proverbs 4:23 NLT)

A few years later I started sixth form and began dating a guy who wasn't a Christian. We met on the hour-and-a-half bus ride I took to school from our village every morning. His name was Gareth and I thought he looked like David Beckham. He made it quite obvious from the first time we spoke that he wanted to be with me and eventually I gave in. Straight after he kissed me for the first time, and I realised he was up for more than I was willing to give, I sat him down to I explain that I was a Christian. I told him that I didn't want to have sex before I got married and he needed to respect that if he wanted to be with me. Later I started to tell him about God and eventually gave him John's gospel to read.

To my surprise, he still wanted to be with me after our chat and we began dating. As the weeks went by I noticed a real change in him. At first he didn't want any commitment in our relationship, but now he looked at things differently and always tried to treat me well. I changed too. He would tell me that he liked me best without makeup. He encouraged me to be myself and respected my faith to the point where he was the one who was stricter about the boundaries I'd put in place than I was.

Through him I learnt that I could bring my faith into a relationship. I saw how I could influence others for good, instead of letting them influence me. I also realised that I wanted to involve God in more of my decisions, particularly when it came to who I spent my time with. Eventually Gareth and I broke up because I knew that I wanted to be with someone who loved God as much as I did, and that this was the most important thing in a relationship.

During this time, my friends and I were running a non-alcoholic bar in town called The Bridge. It was a place for young people to go to on a Saturday night, which was run by Christians who were the same age as them. Each Saturday we'd set up the venue, then when people started arriving, one group would spend the whole evening praying in another room, while others would chat to those who came in. A lot of students from our church would help out with this and it became a pretty exciting place to be.

Among the many that began to attend regularly, I met a tall, dark haired guy called Ethan. Ethan and his friend Rob started coming along almost every week and soon formed a band with some of the other guys who were running The Bridge with me. Sometimes I chatted to them about God and my own faith. Gradually, Ethan became a part of our youth group and the more we spent time together, the more obvious it became that he was attracted to me. I was flattered by his attention. At parties we would often chat and slowly we became best friends.

Ethan grew in his faith and we continued to spend time together. I knew that he liked me and though I enjoyed his friendship and affection, I didn't really feel the same way about him at first. He always did really sweet things for me. The band they had formed started doing gigs, which Rachel and I would go and watch, and I was really touched when he told me he had written one of the songs about me. Eventually, one summer evening, just a few months before he was due to go to university, we discussed our feelings for each other late into the night and then we kissed. This kiss was different to any I had experienced before. As his hands cupped my face, I could really feel the weight of how much he cared about me.

I spent the whole of the next day wondering what to do. I knew I wanted to see him again, but somewhere deep inside I also knew that Ethan was not the one for me. I knew that if I really prayed about it, God would say no. But instead of listening to that gut feeling, which was actually the Holy Spirit, I ignored it. From that moment we started seeing each other secretly, because I was afraid of what our friends would say.

Ethan was a year ahead of me in school and in a few months he would move away to attend Edinburgh University. I had no idea how much I was going to fall for him. I should have listened to what God had said to me at the very beginning, but the idea of being in a relationship with someone who cared for me as much as Ethan did was more appealing than obeying God. In my mind perhaps I thought I could be with Ethan for a while and then break it off at some point in the near future. But, of course, the more intimate our relationship became, the harder it was to pull away, until I found myself disregarding what God had said completely.

"Above all else, guard your heart, for everything you do flows from it." (Proverbs 4:23 NIV)

When we decide to spend time with someone – and really allow them to get to know us in an intimate way – we give them access to our hearts and all the emotions that come with that. The love that I began to feel for Ethan couldn't just be turned on and off. It went much deeper than I thought it would.

The Bible instructs us to guard our hearts. I used to think it was a strange thing to say, but now I know it's the best advice I've ever been given. Our hearts are not something to be thrown around and played with. Our hearts need to be protected, because they are at the very core of who we are, what we do, and how we impact those around us. When we give our heart to someone else, we allow them to influence us, shape who we are. If I had understood this back then, it would have saved me a whole lot of heartache.

When Ethan left for university I was devastated. I really missed him. We wrote letters to each other every day and tried to speak on the halls' phone as much as we could. He came back to visit a couple of weeks later to surprise me and I was so happy to see him. Then, during the Christmas holidays, we spent as much time together as possible. One night as I watched him on stage as his band played, I knew that was it – I had fallen for him hook, line and sinker.

For the past few years all of who I was and the decisions I had made were wrapped around who wanted me. Now my identity was fully placed in this one human being, nineteen year old Ethan, affectionately known by his friends as "Dodge". So caught up was I with how he felt about me, I'd even begun to plan my future around him. Where originally I had thought about applying to universities who specialised in the Arts, now my first choice was Edinburgh University. At the time, I had no idea how shaky my foundations were and in just a few months everything was about to fall apart.

7

REJECTION

I caught the train to Edinburgh on a crisp Friday afternoon. I was on my way to see Ethan for the first time since Christmas. Our time together over the holidays had been so special that I'd been counting the days until I'd see him again and with every day my feelings for him were getting stronger. Now, finally, the day had arrived. Full of excitement I spent the journey picturing what the weekend ahead would be like. But when I met Ethan at the train station, straight away I noticed something wasn't right. He seemed distant and aloof. Suddenly I felt uneasy.

As we walked back to his university halls he told me we would be spending the evening with his friends. They were all girls. They were different from me, he said. They didn't mind letting him see them without any makeup on and, he wondered, why did I? I felt compared, inferior and insecure about him seeing my makeup-free face. All the excitement I had felt on the train had been sapped out of me. I had imagined a perfect weekend with Ethan, now I wasn't sure I was good enough for him any more.

We went to one of the girls' room's that evening. They sat around laughing, singing and joking. I couldn't even pretend to have a good time. I knew something was wrong and I was pretty certain it was me.

The next day he teased me about what I was wearing. He told me that one of his new friends had asked how he had ended up with a girl like me. He said I was too "uncool" for him, since I didn't dress like his university friends. Right then, I would have changed my clothes, my hair, anything, just to make him want me again.

It wasn't until the Saturday evening back in his halls of residence that the words finally fell out of his mouth. "We need to talk," he said. "I'm not sure what I want any more." Before he could say anything else I began to cry; and I mean really cry. All the pent up emotion from the past two days meant I was shaking as tears poured down my face. I felt sick. I wanted to know why, but he couldn't seem to put it into words. He mentioned another girl, who he'd been spending a lot of time with, but everything was so vague. I didn't know what to make of it.

Finally, when the words had all dried up we left his halls of residence to get some food. As we made our way into the city, my eyes were still red from crying. I didn't want to talk with anyone, but Ethan kept bumping into people he knew and it felt like everyone he spoke to knew what was going on between us. The next morning, with everything still undefined, we went to his church.

"The crucible for silver and the furnace for gold, but the Lord tests the heart." (Proverbs 17:3 NLT)

I was still so confused about what had happened between Ethan and I the night before. I had no idea how to work it out. As we began to sing, I cried out to God for help. I remember very clearly we sang:

"A crucible for silver and a furnace for gold, but the Lord tests the heart of His child. Standing in your presence Lord, my passion is for holiness. Lead me to a place where I can sing. Jesus, Holy one. You are my heart's desire. King of kings, my everything. You've set this heart on fire." (Martin Smith)

Looking back, it was like the words of the song had been written for me on that day. As I began to sing this song, I knew that more than anything, I wanted God to be first in my life. He was all I had.

"Fire tests the purity of silver and gold, but a person is tested

by being praised." (Proverbs 27:21 NLT)

For a while my heart had been tested by the praise and affirmation I had been receiving from guys. I hadn't done so well. Instead of looking to God, I had begun to rely on this praise to feel good about who I was. Now it was time for God to intervene. I didn't realise it at the time, but as I sang the words of that song and really meant it, I was asking God to test me once again. To lead me back to a place where He alone was my heart's desire.

There were many words left unspoken between Ethan and I that Sunday. A cloud of uncertainty still hung over us. I was quite obviously still upset as we were saying an awkward goodbye, then just as I was about to get on the train Ethan hugged me and said, taking my hand, "Well, if that is what happens when I'm not sure, I guess we'll need to get married..."

As the train pulled out the station I was even more confused. Was that a proposal?

I went to my home church that evening, tearful and tender. I told my youth leader, Joy, about what had happened at the train station and she looked very concerned. Everything about our relationship was now so unclear. I had no idea what the next few months would hold.

Every day I would wait for Ethan to call me or for a letter to come through the door. But nothing came and I would cry myself to sleep each night, hoping that the phone would ring soon.

A week later it was Valentine's Day and I received a card from Ethan that read, *"Trust in the Lord with all your heart and lean not on your own understanding."* (Proverbs 3:5-6 NIV) Not exactly the message I'd hoped for. That night Rachel and I went to a classical concert and I sobbed all the way through it. I couldn't stop thinking about what had happened between Ethan and I. I knew it was over, yet still I hoped that something would change.

Breaking up with someone is always hard. For me, at this time, it felt like the end of the world. I'd put all my self-worth in the hands of a boy and it had not worked out well. Now there was no one pursuing me and my self-worth hit rock bottom.

The words in the card were not the message I *wanted* to hear, but even though I wasn't ready for it yet, they were the ones I *needed* to hear. I did need to trust God. I needed to look to Him for guidance instead of going my own way. Looking back it is clear to see that God was working, but in the middle of it all it was so very hard to see.

At the same time as all of this, I began to hear back from the universities I had applied to. Week by week, letter after letter hit the mat by our front door. As I opened the envelopes each one said the same word: REJECTION. I was predicted to achieve A's and B's. Why were they all rejecting me?

Three months passed and I hadn't heard a word from Ethan. Then one Saturday, while I was at work, Ethan appeared out of the blue.

"Oi," he said awkwardly.

I looked over, surprised to see him. I was worn out by the past few months – I just wanted some answers now.

"What is going on?" I asked. "Is it over?"

"Yes," he nodded.

We talked for a little while and he tried to explain how he felt. Going to university had changed a lot of things for him. He didn't know what he wanted any more. In fact, he didn't even feel like he knew who he was. I managed to hold it together until he left the shop, then collapsed into tears on one of the ladies who I worked with.

There was no doubt about it, I had been rejected again. Rejection may as well have been written on my forehead.

Those few months were a painful time, but as all my ideas

about the future were wiped off the table, there was space to hear from God again.

Ethan recognised that he didn't really know who he was and the truth is, I didn't know who I was either. In the end, that break up was the best thing that could have happened, because it set me back onto the treasure hunt adventure for my life that God had begun.

As I began to seek God afresh, He quickly reminded me of that time at Spring Harvest when I was 13, when He Had spoken to me about joining Activate. This time I knew that it really was Him speaking to me five years ago – and it was time to be obedient.

As I spoke to one of my youth leaders, Vicky, about all that was happening, she gave me this verse:

"'For I know the plans I have for you,' says the Lord. 'Plans to prosper you and not to harm you. Plans to give you a hope and a future.'" (Jeremiah 29:11 NIV)

I had to trust God. I had no other choice. I was weak and I needed God to show me the way. I applied to Activate and was offered an interview.

8

THE JOURNEY BEGINS

From the other side of the hall I felt their eyes on me as I arrived at the church in Worcester. Here was the team I was hoping to join and I already felt intimidated by them. I could hear my heart pounding nervously through my chest as I sat down on the wooden chair before the interview panel. My Dad and I had left our house early that morning to drive down to my interview and audition with Activate and now it was time to start.

But before they even began to interview me, Damian, the Director of Activate, started by praying: "Thank you, God, that you know the plans you have for Tamsin and that they are plans to prosper and not to harm her."

He had prayed from the same verse that Vicky, my youth leader, had given me just a few weeks earlier. I was amazed. It was only the second time I had heard that verse. My nerves eased a little as I was reminded that this was where God wanted me to be. All along He had a plan. He had shown me the clues along the way. It was me who had become distracted and wandered off until I was so lost I couldn't see the way out. But He had intervened and used all that rejection for His good and now I was so glad that He had.

A few days later, I was offered a place on the team and, of course, I accepted.

I was still cut up over my break up with Ethan and holding onto a bit of hope that things could go back to how they used to be. I had planned our future together and persuaded myself that he was the one I would marry. This ideal was further dashed when Rachel called me that week after she had spent the day with Ethan and told me that she had spoken to him about our relationship. It was definitely over. He didn't want to be with me, there was no going back.

The next months were hard. My feelings for Ethan didn't just go away. I still thought I loved him, but also I loved the idea of having someone who loved me. Now there was no one showing me that kind of attention any more. For so long I had summed up what I was worth by whether I was pretty enough, clever enough, interesting enough to attract such attention – or according to what guys thought of me. But now it was gone. I was stripped of everything that I had defined myself by and this was the time to be rebuilt.

God is our Father and even when it doesn't feel like it, He is always working for our good. Sometimes He uses painful situations in the most surprising ways.

Near the very beginning of the Bible we read about the life of Moses. Right from the very start of his life it was clear that God wanted to use him in a special way. Moses was born to Israelite parents at a time when the Israelites were slaves in Egypt. When Moses was born, the Pharaoh had decided that the population of Israel was too large, so he ordered a massacre of all boys under the age of three. To save his life Moses was hidden in a basket by his family, which floated down the river and was discovered by the Pharaoh's daughter, who was an Egyptian. Much to everyone's surprise she immediately took Moses in and decided that she would raise him as her own child in the palace.

What a mix of emotions his family must have felt. God had spared Moses' life, but now he would grow up like an Egyptian, in the house of the very man who had enslaved them. Why would God rescue Moses in this way? And why would God want Moses to grow up in a palace with strangers and a leader who wanted to kill baby boys? Surely it would have been better for him to grow up in his own family?

But God had a much bigger plan in mind. Not only did growing up in the palace save Moses' life, it also meant he grew up as a free man, unlike the rest of his people, who were still living as slaves. What's more, he was treated as royalty and taught to behave as royals should. Growing up in the palace gave Moses a different perspective and a different way of thinking – so that he would be able to lead the Israelites out of slavery and into freedom.

Sometimes God takes us through situations and circumstances so that we gain a different perspective. He positions us so that we can fulfil the plans and purposes He has for us. God had plans to use all the unique experiences I had growing up, but some of my thinking needed to be changed if I was to do all the things He was calling me to do. Through all this pain and rejection God showed me that I had defined myself by all the wrong things, seeking affirmation in man's affection and academic achievement. As I began to realise this, God gave me a different perspective.

Each of us grows up with earthly parents and faces earthly situations, but in order for us to live as God intended, we need a different perspective. We need to know our identity in Him before we can live as God has planned for us to live. Knowing the truth about who we are changes the way we think and the way we act.

The Bible says we are children of the living God, royalty in fact. Jesus is our king and we are His family.

In the midst of the rejection I'd faced, God was calling me out, reminding me through the verse in Jeremiah of the plans He had for me, reminding me that He had given me clues along the way. God in His grace often uses the mistakes we make along the journey to grow character in us.

Through his experiences God had given Moses a different

perspective from the rest of the Israelites, but he still didn't quite have the mind set God wanted him to have. When Moses was still living in Pharaoh's house he saw an Egyptian beating one of his fellow Israelites. It's the first time in the Bible we see that Moses is affected by the injustice of the slavery of his people. He gets so angry about what he sees that when no one is looking, he kills that Egyptian and hides him in the sand (Exodus 2:11-12).

He felt passion for his people and a righteous anger at the unfair way they were being treated, but he acted on it in the wrong way. I think deep inside, even Moses knew it was the wrong thing to do. The next day when he tried to settle an argument between two Israelites, one of them mocked him saying, *"Who made you ruler over us? Are you thinking of killing me like you killed the Egyptian?"* (Exodus 2:13-14 NIV). He had been found out. Terrified of the consequences, Moses ran away into the wilderness.

For Moses it must have felt like it was all over. He'd tried to do something to save his people, but it didn't work. Maybe he felt stupid for even thinking that he could make a difference when he realised that his own people didn't accept him. But even when he ran away God was still working behind the scenes. In the wilderness God gave Moses a community and a place where he had space to hear the voice of God.

Growing up in a palace had changed his perspective. It showed him what life could be like as a free person and helped him to understand his royal identity. But in the wilderness God grew his character, changed his thinking and prepared him for his role as "rescuer".

Like Moses, each of us has our own story in which God is working behind the scenes. He knows everything about us and works in the very detail of our lives.

He knew what was needed for Moses to take hold of his destiny and lead his people into freedom. He knew what I needed before I could see myself the way He saw me, and begin to take hold of my destiny. He knows what is needed for you.

In the wilderness God reminded Moses of who he was called to be and showed him how he was to set his people free. God will often take us through "wilderness" situations where He shows us that our perspective needs to change. Without this change of perspective we think that we can do things on our own, like Moses did when he killed that Egyptian, but God had a far better plan.

God needed to take me through what felt like a wilderness so that He could have the space to remind me of who He had called me to be. I needed a change of perspective to see myself the way God saw me.

For me, rock bottom was the beginning of a whole new and much better adventure.

9

WHO I REALLY AM

The last few months of Sixth Form flew by and the much talked about graduation ball was fast approaching. Still jaded by all the rejection I'd faced, I really didn't want to go. My friend, Hope, finally persuaded me to come with her and my Mum, wanting to encourage me, bought me a beautiful black lace dress to wear. Then just a few hours before I was due to go and get ready with a group of friends, Hope called to say she couldn't make it. I was already low and this felt like one more rejection. I didn't want to disappoint my Mum, but I couldn't face going to the ball without Hope, so I lied.

I left my house in the dress she had bought me, my face and hair made up, and met up with one of my close friends, Andy, instead. He knew about everything that had happened over the past few months and had been a rock through all of it. I spent the evening at his house, then late that night he walked me home so that it would seem to my parents and aunty, who was staying, like I had gone to the ball.

I hated lying to them, but I didn't want them to know how deeply I was still hurting.

So much of my worth was tied up in who wanted me and now the answer really seemed to be no one. God had been removing all the things in my life that I had relied upon to answer the questions I had about my identity. I had been hurt and now I was consumed by all that had happened to me. If I was ever going to move forward, I needed to find a way to let go of the past.

But how do you let go?

When we've been hurt, rejected or disappointed, we can't just bury the pain we feel or pretend it's not there. That never works. The pain we're trying to hide will only grow to become more painful, often manifesting itself in other ways as we try to deal with it, causing us to be even more hurt.

At the beginning of the summer holidays I went to visit friends in Devon, then straight after that, Rachel and I went to the Lake District together. As I spent time with close friends away from home I was able to let go of those things I had held on to and turn to God.

Both through conversations and time spent on my own, God kept reminding me of the cross. How he sent Jesus, His only Son to die there, carrying our pain so that we could be forgiven. All of it handed over at the cross. In my mind I saw myself at the foot of the cross, laying down each bit of pain and leaving it there until there was nothing left to bury.

After the Lake District, I had signed up to spend two weeks volunteering, first at New Wine and then at the first week of Soul Survivor. Following this I'd planned to stay for the second week of the conference with my friend, Hope. By the time the second week of Soul Survivor arrived, I was ready to leave all the pain behind. I went forward for prayer at almost every meeting and, for some reason, there was one lady would always find me amongst the crowd and pray with me. It was like God had placed her there for me as I let all the hurt, the disappointment, the pain, the rejection out. As I began to open my heart to God and give my pain to Him, He showed me that I needed to let go and forgive some people who had hurt me.

"Forgiveness starts here … Forgiveness liberates the soul … It removes fear, that is why it is such a powerful weapon … The past is the past, we look to the future." (Nelson Mandela, Invictus)

To move into our future we need to let go of the past. Quite often, a key way to let go of our past is by forgiving. There have been times when I've been hurt and it's been really hard to forgive, but by not forgiving, I've been the one held back. There is no point letting shackles of unforgiveness chain us to the past. We need to move forward.

"For the Lord is the Spirit and wherever the Spirit of the Lord is, there is freedom." (2 Corinthians 3:17 NLT)

Once I'd been able forgive those who hurt me and hand my pain over to Jesus there was space for God to begin to write His truth in my heart again, and gently He did this.

I didn't realise it, but I had been held captive to the lie that I was only worth something if a guy found me attractive. But as the Holy Spirit worked in my heart, He set me free from believing that lie. One night I was on my own in my tent reading the Bible when God began to speak to me powerfully through Psalm 139:

"You made all the delicate, inner parts of my body and knit me together in my mother's womb. Thank you for making me so wonderfully complex! Your workmanship is marvellous—how well I know it. You watched me as I was being formed in utter seclusion, as I was woven together in the dark of the womb. You saw me before I was born. Every day of my life was recorded in your book. Every moment was laid out before a single day had passed. How precious are your thoughts about me, O God. They cannot be numbered! I can't even count them; they outnumber the grains of sand! And when I wake up, you are still with me!" (Psalm 139:13-18 NLT)

It was as though He was reading it aloud to me, gently but powerfully speaking the truth into the very core of who I was. I could hear the hum of chatting from tents all around me, but I didn't want leave my tent. I was fixated on the words and they were changing my heart.

I had read these words before, but it was now that they finally started to register with me. My worth was not in who wanted me or what I achieved in life. None of that mattered when I truly began to understand what it meant that God had created me. He had crafted every part of me. He knew me and loved me as I was. Thankfulness about the way He made me rose up in my throat as the truth finally dawned on me.

He saw me before I was born. His thoughts about me were numerous and He was with me! As I let go of all the pain I was carrying, my perspective was able to change and now I could see myself as He saw me.

A few guys showed interest in me while I was away that summer, but it was different this time. The hole in me that had desperately needed to be filled by a guy's affirmation was now filled by God's love for me, as the revelation about who I was really deepened.

I spent the last month of my summer holiday back home, working at three jobs in order to raise money for my year with Activate, but now things felt so different. I saw Ethan before I left for Activate and though I still held out a little bit of hope that Ethan and I might get back together, I knew that my worth was not wrapped up in how he saw me any more.

What's more, this experience of God's truth transforming the way I thought about myself gave me faith that God could do the same for my friends – and for those in schools across the country I would meet as I started my year on Activate. No longer did I just feel frustrated by the struggles my friends were having. I had my own story of how my relationship with God had impacted the struggles I had faced. I could see that my worth had been in all the wrong things. I had learnt how to let go the hard way and how to surrender myself to Him.

Acclaimed author Marianne Williamson wrote in her book *A*

Return to Love the inspiring verse:

"Our deepest fear is not that we are inadequate. Our deepest fear is that we are powerful beyond measure. We ask ourselves, 'Who am I to be brilliant, gorgeous, talented, and fabulous?' Actually, who are you not to be? You are a child of God. Your playing small does not serve the world. There's nothing enlightened about shrinking so that other people don't feel insecure around you. We are born to make manifest the glory of God that is within us. And as we let our own light shine, we unconsciously give other people permission to do the same. As we are liberated from our own fear, our presence automatically liberates others."

If we really see ourselves the way God sees us it changes everything. As we allow Him continually to reveal His love to us, as we spend time in His presence and reading His word, what He says will become more embedded in our thinking. We were created to shine, not shrink back. We were made to live liberated lives, not to be held back. We can take on false thinking which says we need to somehow make ourselves smaller, to fit in, but instead we need to get God's perspective. When we discover for ourselves that the God of heaven is pleased with how He uniquely made us, we'll stop worrying about what other people think, or shrinking ourselves back to make them happy, and we will just get on with fully being ourselves.

"Let's just go ahead and be what we were made to be, without enviously or pridefully comparing ourselves with each other, or trying to be something we aren't." (Romans 12:6 MSG)

In the discovery of all of this truth about how God saw me, I decided, and I told God, "Let the next guy I fall for be the guy you have chosen for me. I'm done with trying to work this out myself. Let me only fall in love with someone because of their love for you."

No longer was I craving the past or for things or myself to be different. Finally, I had surrendered to God. I was ready for His adventure.

Section 2
AWAKENING

Birds are born with an innate instinct to fly, yet no bird is born with this ability. Birds learn as they watch from the nest until it's their time to try for themselves. With encouragement and perseverance they are then ready to take their first steps into flight.

10

OBEDIENCE

5,6,7,8... The music started and I found myself on a smoke filled stage dancing in front of an entire school. "How did I get here?" I wondered. Looking out, I saw a sea of faces staring right back at me, as though they were waiting for me to impress them. I did my best to perform the dance routine I had learnt a few weeks earlier, but having never had a strong sense of rhythm, I think I ended up looking more like a chicken than anything else.

Yet here I was, dancing during my gap year, doing what God had clearly told me to do when I was thirteen.

"I can't dance," I remember saying at my audition, stumbling through the dance moves they tried to teach me. I really wanted to sing, not dance! Ironically, I was assigned more dances than the rest of the team. The performance schedule was set for the year and I was completely out of my comfort zone.

"Well God," I thought begrudgingly, "if this is what you have planned, you know best." I secretly hoped this meant I would turn into an incredible dancer. Unfortunately that didn't happen, but He did have purpose in my dancing. God was teaching me about obedience. Little by little I learned not to worry about myself or how I looked. Instead I focused on God and let this dancing that I was so uncomfortable with become my obedient sacrifice of worship to Him. As I began to do this, the sea of faces stopped being so daunting. Instead, God began to show me how He saw them: thousands upon thousands of young people, in the valley of decision, and He was calling me to reach out to them.

Even though I was awake to the purpose of why God had told me to do this year, still it was not always what I expected it to be. It was full of challenges and there were times I seriously questioned whether I was in the right place. I kept a journal during this year, here's what I wrote a couple of weeks into the year.

Monday 20th September 1999:

I am going to focus on God, friendship and developing the talents He has given me. He will sharpen them up. I have to remember the word Alison gave me before I came here: "God wants me here and He has appointed me to be here. He will never leave or forsake me."

Wednesday 22nd September

I found it hard as some Directors of YFC were watching us perform yesterday and I felt rubbish. I don't do anything special. I wish I could sing leads. But I have to remember that God has it all in His hands and I need to be patient. He will fulfil His promises to me. He needs to equip me. He has perfect timing and I trust Him.

Thursday 19th October

Well, first day in school – early start. It is bizarre. I am staying in my first host home. The guy we are staying with leads the church. The church here is so spiritual, they pray all the time. I feel inadequate, like we are this mischievous, selfish, unorganised team who thinks they are great, who wandered into these people's lives to do what? What are we doing? Showing the love of Jesus with our behaviour? I want to be pure, integral and to shine; to be a woman of God.

God was using each challenge to test my obedience and further position the pieces of the vision He had already placed within me. Would I stick with it and trust Him or would I walk away? Then there was Nick and with him came another challenge in obedience.

Thursday 23rd September

Tonight I felt so alone and out of it, having been struggling with dancing all day. I just wanted to run out of the room through the whole evening. Then at the end, finally, I just walked out and started to cry. I walked through the grass to the bench. I said to God please send someone if you want to. I heard footsteps and then Nick was there asking if I was alright. Seeing I was crying, he sat down and put his arm around me and we talked for ages. He was feeling the same as me and it was amazing the way God brought us together at that point. We prayed and talked and prayed. He has such integrity. As we were talking about difficult situations he would stop and just pray. I really respect that. I praise you God that you brought him to me tonight and for the prayer and talks we had. Thank you.

As I started the team, I quickly formed a friendship with Nick and in October, when we were performing at an event in Birmingham Cathedral, I felt God draw my attention to him as he was chatting to a homeless man. I looked over at him and felt God say, "That is your husband." For a split second I questioned: "Do you mean Nick, or the homeless man?" I called my friend Andy from home and told him what had happened. "God doesn't speak like this, does He?" Andy said he thought I had heard God.

The next month, I found out that Ethan had a new girlfriend and I was gutted. But God challenged my obedience again: "Tamsin what did I say? I have told you who your husband is."

Still I wasn't convinced that God could speak like this, so in my uncertainty I said to Him, "If you really want me to marry

Nick, let him come to me by the end of the day with a word of encouragement." I waited and at 6pm that day, Nick gave me a note. Inside he had written a verse from Psalm 30:5:

"In the evening there will be sadness and tears, in the morning there will be rejoicing."

I had asked God for confirmation; He had answered.

Sunday 5th December

I went for prayer at this event called Revive. Said I wanted a passion and hunger for God. Claire had two pictures for me: the first was that God totally meant for me to be in Activate. That God is so pleased with me. The second was that God is keeping my heart, guarding it. He holds the key and he says to me "Wait. I don't want anyone to come along. I am holding the key for someone really special who will come in my timing and I want you to have fun and concentrate on what you are doing. Know that I hold the key and have that for you and no one else can touch it.

Later Nick said that he had been praying and felt God wanted to remind me of Jeremiah 29:11: "For I know the plans I have for you, plans to prosper you, not to harm you."

God had spoken to me about the man I would marry. He was speaking to me about what the future would hold. But He had also put me in an environment where I was not allowed to start any new relationships or change the way things happened now. I had to be obedient and let the journey progress as God was leading.

"Be still in the presence of the Lord and wait patiently for him to act." (Psalm 37:7 NIV)

When we learn how be still and to wait for God, we begin to realise that life is not about what we can achieve, it's about God working His purposes through us. It's not easy to be obedient when God asks us to wait, it goes against everything in us that wants to know, see or understand. But there's an incredible sense of peace when we let go and trust God. It is so powerful learning to just "be" in God's presence in a situation and trusting Him to lead and to act. When we are obedient and wait for Him to act, He does something far better in us, and in the situation, than we could do on our own.

I needed to trust. There were so many reasons not to, but God had clearly spoken to me and shown me His plan. I needed to concentrate on the year ahead of me and trust what God was doing through it, even when I couldn't see it or even understand.

As a team we travelled to a different place each week. We'd perform in schools across the area and then invite the young people to a concert on the Friday night where we would share the gospel with them. It sounds exciting, but in reality we spent a lot of time setting up and packing down for each performance. We worked hard. When we got sick, we took a bucket back stage to vomit in between scenes. The show had to go on!

As we travelled from school to school, I encountered so many young people who were struggling:

Wednesday 20th October 1999
Met a girl called Rachel today. She was crying. Someone had hit her at school.

Friday 5th November 1999
Prayed for a girl Bethany who felt suicidal.

Saturday 13th November 1999
I spoke with three girls. One asked me, "What is it like to have someone love you?"

Friday 26th November 1999
*Spoke with a girl called Christina about becoming a Christian.
I feel like I am rubbish. I don't know what to say or anything. I
don't know how to explain Christianity – feel conscious of doing
it wrong.*

These were just a few of the young people I came across during
that year. The more I saw the hurting around me, the more I
saw that they needed Jesus. But also they needed someone to
support and help them to overcome their struggles. Five minutes
to try to explain Christianity and pray for them just didn't seem
enough in the light of the challenges they faced. More often
than not, it seemed that we would leave them without seeing
any resolution. We'd just have to trust that someone else would
come along to help them. But a lot of the time, it seemed that
the youth workers we met felt ill-equipped to properly help
these young people. There had to be more.

Each frustration held room for a possibility, for a new dream
to be birthed. There was more at stake than just getting caught
up in guys and relationships – there were lives that we were
encountering each day. Thousands of people searching for hope.
As I looked to God in this time, a desire in me began to grow to
see something more to support these young people.

It wasn't just in the schools that I saw this need, a lot of my
team mates were struggling with similar issues too. So many
of the team were caught up in the need for affirmation and
were meeting this need through being on stage, just like I had
previously found affirmation through different guys' attentions.
I knew first hand how dangerous this was and it broke my heart
to see it. There was so much more I knew God wanted to do, but
I had to trust Him through the process He was taking me on and

learn along the way.

"This vision-message is a witness pointing to what's coming. It aches for the coming – it can hardly wait! And it doesn't lie. If it seems slow in coming, wait. It's on its way. It will come right on time." (Habakkuk 2:3 MSG)

There was vision brewing in my heart and at the right time it would surface. All I had to do was be obedient, be still and wait for God to act.

11

THE PROMISE

With one last look at my bedroom I closed the door. From downstairs I could hear my parents calling. It was time to go. I squeezed into the car, piled high with my belongings and we began our journey. So much had happened over the past few weeks, I struggled to remember how exactly we had got here. Just a month ago I was with Activate, performing at a huge outreach event called Message 2000. I smiled to myself as I remembered how Nick and I had spent several hours making dinner for the group. Damian, our Director, was fuming when we had taken most of the afternoon to prepare the meal. He wanted to know why it had taken three hours to prepare a sausage casserole that should have been done in half an hour. He was well aware of the feelings we had for each other, but romantic relationships between team members were not allowed and it was his job to make sure we didn't break the rules.

As the last day came, we said our goodbyes. There were tears for some but, honestly, I was excited about finishing. I was going home to York that evening and then Nick would be joining me the next day. That car journey was the reverse of the one we were taking today.

I met Nick at the station, nervous to see what was about to unfold between us. Wondering again if I had read the signs all wrong and he actually just wanted to be my friend.

But then he kissed me and every doubt in my mind disappeared. He really did have feelings for me. We spent a few days in York together and then flew to Jersey to join my family on holiday.

It was a perfect week. Beaches, sun, surf and evenings by a lighthouse where the sky stretched out like a starry-jewelled carpet above us. It scared me how much I had grown to care for Nick during our past year on team together. I began to realise how vulnerable I was, because I wasn't in control of how this would work out. I had spent a year, day in day out, with this guy. Our hearts had connected over so much as we shared our passion for God and our desire to give our lives fully to Him. We didn't want to live ordinary lives, tied down by mortgages and 9-5 jobs. Instead we wanted to be ready to go wherever God sent us. Now I realised that this was what I wanted more than anything, to live out God's adventures with Nick.

The vulnerability of falling for someone again was almost too much. I'd had my heart broken before, was I really ready to be here again?

My heart had not become hardened by my last breakup, but I had felt the searing pain of rejection. Instead of responding to this rejection by locking my heart away so it was impenetrable, I had given it to God. It hadn't been easy, but I had come to realise that this was the safest place for my heart to be. I trusted that as I kept my heart soft and vulnerable in God's hands He would show me the right time to love again.

And this time was different. I had prayed earnestly to God, asking that the next guy I fell for would be the one He had chosen for me. I knew I was falling for Nick and that meant my heart was at risk of being broken again. In fact, everything I could see said it wouldn't work, because nothing about our circumstances was certain. Nick was from Australia, his visa was due to expire and now that Activate was finished he would have to leave the UK soon. Everything looked impossible for us, but I knew that this time God was in it and I had to choose to hold on to what we had heard Him say.

A fly buzzed at the car window, interrupting my thoughts. As we tried to shoo it out of the window we laughed as we recalled a day on our holiday when I was plagued by a relentless buzzing noise. I was trying to work out where it was coming from when, to my horror, I realised it was me. I was buzzing! Without thinking I began to pull my clothes off in front of my entire family. Not knowing what else to do, Nick quickly left the room, afraid I would strip completely to escape the wasp trapped inside my jumper. We laughed together for a while at the memory and then fell back into silence. No one wanted to talk about how that week had ended.

On the last day of our holiday, Nick and I had taken a trip to St Malo in France. We spent the day exploring the wall-surrounded city and laughing at my failed attempts to communicate coherently in French. On the journey back we had stupidly argued over a shell that Nick had bought me as a gift to remember the day. Perhaps we both knew that there was an unspoken question mark over our future together. With the tension still hanging in the air, we walked through immigration to meet my Dad who was there to collect us. But at passport control we were separated. I had a British passport, Nick had an Australian one – an unwelcome reminder of the reality that we were from opposite sides of the world. I went through quickly, expecting Nick to be right behind me, but he wasn't. He had been held for questioning.

Peering through the gate I strained to hear the conversation between Nick and the immigration officer. "What are you doing in the UK?" she asked. Nick began to explain that he had a visa for voluntary work and had been working with Youth for Christ for the past year.

"And when did this voluntary work finish?" she interrupted,

clearly not interested in small talk. Nick, unperturbed and always quick to call anyone mate, explained cheerfully how the work had finished a few weeks ago, but he had met me during the year and believed he would marry me. He then proceeded, in retrospect unwisely, to ask her for advice on how to go about this as an Australian citizen. Red flags went up everywhere and Nick was taken to a side room for further questioning. Jersey, as one of the Channel Islands, is a hot spot for illegal entry into the UK and, as a result, is extremely cautious about allowing foreign citizens onto the island. In this case, the immigration officer questioning Nick had now discovered that the purpose for Nick's voluntary worker visa had expired. He currently had no job or income and had admitted he wanted to marry a UK citizen. In her mind, he was highly likely to try and stay in the country illegally.

It became her mission to ensure that Nick would leave the UK as soon as possible. She proceeded to ask him for proof that he had the funds to purchase a ticket back to Australia and then called my Dad through to certify and sign that he would ensure Nick left the country within a month. We left the port heavy-hearted, the 13th September stamped in our minds and on Nick's passport as the date he must leave the country. The cloud above our heads had darkened. Nick had just one month left in the UK before he had to go home.

The car jolted and my head bumped against the window, reminding me that it was three weeks later now and we weren't on holiday any more. We were on our way to Liverpool, where I would be starting university, and the 13th September was looming.

12

NOTHING IS IMPOSSIBLE

Nick and I had visited Liverpool with Activate a few months before. Our team had been booked by a church called Frontline to go into schools in the surrounding area. On this trip, I met Claire. She was our contact from Frontline's Real Life schools team. When I told her I was moving to Liverpool to start university, she set about the task of helping me find a place to live. Shortly afterwards I was introduced to Charlotte and Louise, who had a vacant room in the house they shared. It seemed everything had fallen into place.

But now, actually on the journey to Liverpool, the reality set in. I was moving into a house in the middle of a concrete jungle with two girls who were practically strangers.

I should have been full of excitement. I was starting a course at the Liverpool Institute of Performing Arts (LIPA), the place I knew God wanted me to be. But all I felt was fear. The closer we came to Liverpool, the harder I tried to focus my mind on all God had done to show me He wanted me in this city.

Waiting nervously in the foyer on my audition day at LIPA, I had heard a voice within me, telling me that this was where I would be. I was beginning to realise that this could be God speaking to me, but throughout that day I questioned this. The lecturers welcomed us to our audition by reminding us that there were only 30 places available on the course and many of those had already been given away. The competition was fierce and only two of us from that group of 20 would end up being offered a place. Later that day, as I waited in the corridor to be called for my audition, I heard the loud cry of an orgasm being acted out before the panel that I was due to face next. Doubts clouded my mind. Was this the sort of thing they wanted? My audition piece was an innocent and quirky adaptation of a poem from *Under Milk Wood* by Dylan Thomas. Was this really where God wanted me to be? I was so different to everyone else, how would I fit in here?

A few weeks later I received an unconditional offer from LIPA. Still I wondered, did God really want me to go there? I had also been offered a place at a university in London, which in some ways seemed much more appealing.

I was back with the rest of the Activate team in Bournemouth when I finally made the decision about LIPA. We were helping at a Christian Conference called Easter People and Jackie Pullinger was one of the main speakers. Jackie Pullinger is a missionary who works in Hong Kong with drug addicts and triad gang members. I had read her book previously and was inspired by the way she had stepped out and followed God to Hong Kong. I loved how brave she was and how much she depended on God in all she did. I wanted to be like that.

One evening during a meeting in the youth venue I had been assigned to, Jackie was speaking. That night was different from the others. You could feel the presence of God like a thick blanket covering the room. I remember praying, "God, I want to go wherever you want me to be. Please make it clear and show me where that is." And although God had already spoken to me, He was gracious enough to make it so clear that I could not doubt it any more.

Jackie stood up at the front of the room and began to speak about following God's call: "God may be calling you to be a missionary like me," she said. My response was, "Yes Lord, is this it? Should I go and be a missionary?"

"Or God could be calling you to University..."

The words hit me hard. Suddenly I knew God was speaking to me. Jackie continued, "God could be calling you to Outer Mongolia or God could be calling you to Liverpool."

My eyes filled with tears. Of all the places she could have chosen, she said Liverpool. We were in Bournemouth, in the South of England, the other end of the country from Liverpool, a small city up north. That was it. I made the decision to go to Liverpool.

God had said it. I reminded myself as I looked out at the grey sky and bleak hilly countryside racing by. We were at the highest point on our journey through the Pennines, England's highest motorway. Here, the motorway splits and between the east and westbound motorway lanes is a lonely farmhouse wedged between the two sides of fast motorway traffic. Like the farmhouse, I felt wedged between two things. I knew that God had called me to LIPA, but at the same time there was Nick, where would he be? I reached over and found his hand.

Nick, who I believed God had told me I would marry. Nick, who I had been going out with for a little over a month. Nick, who was leaving in a week. Overwhelmed with this feeling of desolation, my mind drifted back to February. Halfway through our year with Activate, we were performing in schools across Devon and Cornwall. Touring across the country, we often stayed with host families whilst we worked in the surrounding areas. This time I was staying with Dee from the team, who was driving our mini bus for the week. Nick and another guy from our team called Matt were staying nearby, but the rest of the team were hosted in farmhouses a thirty minute drive away. Each day that week Matt would sit at the front of the bus chatting to Dee, while Nick and I had the rare opportunity to talk alone.

The conversations stretched out through the week, both of us alluding to our feelings for each other, but never quite making it clear. Towards the end of the week we performed in a church hall in the depths of rural Devon. It was a place that could only be found by counting trees. Halfway through the concert, between dances, Nick finally said that the way he felt about me would never change. In that moment I realised for the first time that he felt the same way about me as I did about him. As the conversations progressed we discovered that, before we had joined the Activate team, both of us had been given words by trusted friends about meeting the person we would marry during this year.

Both our hearts were set on following God and each morning we would seek God in prayer asking Him to reveal His heart and plans for us. Through these times of prayer we had separately sensed God speak to us about marrying the other. I wrestled with this thought often. Then, when a friend of mine told me that someone else she knew had felt God say she would marry Nick, I doubted myself even more. All this time Nick was struggling with similar thoughts. Without knowing, Nick and I both continued to pray that if God really did want us to be together, He would confirm it. And He did.

Yet now, like that farmhouse between two motorway lanes, I was positioned between two promises that seemed like they were heading full speed in opposite directions. In just one week, the man God wanted me to be with would be sent back to the other side of the world and I would start my course at university in Liverpool. There was no certainty that Nick would get a visa to return. He had already been granted two visas to live in the UK and without a job lined up it looked unlikely that he would receive another. Neither of us felt that being in a long distance relationship for three years was a viable option. I remember saying to a friend that I could always move to Australia if Nick couldn't come back. But I knew God had called me to LIPA for the next three years and I didn't want to be disobedient to what God had said. The circumstances made it look impossible, but I had to remind myself of who God was and of all the times He had been faithful to me.

I was in that car going to Liverpool because God had told me to, not because I had chosen the city. In fact, the idea of living in Liverpool scared me. I just had to trust.

That first week of inductions at university passed quickly and on the 13th of September, Nick left in the small hours of the morning to get his flight. I knew the day was coming when Nick would leave, but I wasn't prepared for how it would make me feel. I couldn't eat. I felt physically sick. I remember phoning my previous youth leader, Joy, in floods of tears at five o'clock the morning he left. I felt like someone had blacked out all the light and left me alone in a dark, empty room. I had opened up my heart to Nick, given in to the raw vulnerability of love and now he was gone. My dad came to visit, countless friends chatted on the phone, but nothing really helped.

It was my birthday the week after Nick left and he had left some parcels under my bed. One contained a hoody that I had seen a few weeks before and really liked. I put it on straight away and from that day, I wore it often. A few days later on the bus to a lecture, I reached my hand into the front pocket and found a note that Nick had left there.

It read: "This is my last note. But it comes with all my love. If this is meant to be, then nothing can come between us. I love you. Nick." A tear ran down my cheek. Suddenly it felt like he was with me again.

University was in full swing when one weekend Heather, a

friend from Activate, came to visit me. She lived in Manchester and had met Nick at the airport the day he left. Having seen how heartbroken he was to leave me, it felt like she had more understanding of our relationship than anybody else at the time. As we talked about Nick, she encouraged me to have faith in what God had said to us. Before she left, she put a sign up by my bed which read: "Nothing is Impossible with God". Her faith in the fact that we had heard God, and that He would work it out, challenged me to look to God for the strength to keep going. Friends were good, but God alone knew. Friends had the habit of trying to prepare me for the worst, but I needed to remember and trust in the times that God had been faithful to His word, despite how impossible things had looked.

I made myself look at Scripture, at all the things that happened that were impossible without God. How Mary was told she would give birth to the Son of God, and she believed God, and it happened. How Abraham and Sarah were told they would have a son, even though they were too old and it was physically impossible. As I studied the Bible, I found strength in the stories of people who believed God despite the impossibility they were facing and began to trust that God could do the same for Nick and me.

There is nothing like learning to trust when you have no other option but to trust. I had no reason to believe that Nick and I would be together, apart from what God had said to us. Yet instead of focusing on all the reasons why it wouldn't work, I began to put my hope in God's word. As I continued to do this my faith that He would work things out grew. This faith helped me to not just cope with the uncertainties I was facing, but grow through them too. I became stronger and more resilient in spite of them. When we choose to seek God in difficult times in our lives, He can use the challenges to help us grow.

And God was faithful to his promise!

A few months later I stood in Manchester Airport's arrival lounge waiting for Nick, who had received a two year visa to live in the UK. I ran to meet him as he came through the gates, surfboard on his back. We clung to each other on the train home, amazed at this promised fulfilled. This experience of hearing from God and seeing an impossible situation turn around fuelled in me a greater determination to listen to God's word in every situation. Instead of looking at what the circumstances said, I learnt to look to God's word and have faith in His ability to do what He promised.

At that moment everything felt perfect. We felt untouchable at the beginning of a sunny new chapter of life together in Liverpool. Little did we know what dark sadness awaited Nick just a few weeks away.

13

PROCESSING PAIN

The streetlights lit up a gloomy night outside my university building. Tired and bored, I stared out of the window waiting impatiently for my compulsory lighting and sound course to finish. I had no interest in the technicalities of lighting or sound and spent every session watching the minute hand inch its way across the clock face until it was time to leave. That night, Nick was coming to pick me up, so I was even more impatient than usual for the class to finish. The fact that he was even here in the same country as me still gave me a thrill. Only weeks ago it had seemed impossible.

The class finally ended and I was first out the door. My footsteps echoed down the ornate staircase that twisted around the Paul McCartney auditorium as I ran to the foyer to meet Nick. Perhaps we'd go for a drink or maybe a walk through the city streets. In my mind I was already with him. Then, as I walked through security and to the door, I saw a couple I recognised from our church coming towards me.

I was a little confused. Why were they here? Before I had a chance to think about where Nick was, they put their arms around me. "Nick's not coming," they said, as they ushered me out into the dark car park and into their car. "He's just heard some news ... his brother has died."

"What?" I gasped as shock hit me.

I felt sick. I rummaged in my bag to find my phone, which I hadn't checked for the last hour. There were missed calls and messages from Nick's housemates telling me that Nick needed me, asking me to come to his home. Questions raced through my mind. Which brother was it? Nick was the oldest in his family and he cared a great deal for all of his siblings. He had found it so hard to say goodbye to them when he left Australia. How would he cope with this news? What could I do or say to help? And why had this happened when he was so far away? How could he be there for them during this time if they were all in Australia and he was here in the UK? How would he ever get over this?

I arrived at his house to find him in the kitchen, sitting in silent shock. He repeated, almost robotically, the phone conversation he'd had with his Mum. That night people from our church came round to the house trying to show support, but what could any of us do? We hadn't ever met his brothers. How could any of us really identify with the loss he felt? There was nothing to say that could ease the pain of what had had happened.

The next hours, days and weeks were painful as I watched Nick begin to work out how to grieve for his much loved stepbrother David, who had taken his own life by driving his parents' car into a wall at the local police station.

I listened to Nick as he rehearsed the guilt he felt for not being there, wishing he hadn't left Australia; all the times he irrationally blamed himself for what had happened. We began to question whether he really should have come to England when he did; whether the miracle visa, was in fact a big mistake. In Melbourne, a few weeks earlier, Nick had spent the day with David and some friends at a local field near their home. They had driven to this field because it was private land and spent the afternoon racing the car along the wet field and doing doughnuts, spinning the car around in fast circles in the wet dirt. The day was full of laughter. But beyond the laughter, David had seemed angry.

Then, on the 23rd November as dawn broke over their family home, Nick's step-dad, John, and his mum, Kirsten, woke to the buzzing of their intercom. They answered it to discover that the police were at the door, bringing the tragic news of David's untimely death.

How does any parent hear that kind of news about their son? How can any sister or brother bear to witness the body of their brother and friend after it has been involved in such an incident? Nick spent many hours cruelly questioning himself. If he had been at home would it still have happened? Could he have changed anything? He longed for something that would help him make sense of what was happening to his family. He was distant, withdrawn and he struggled to do things that he enjoyed.

As Nick replayed these thoughts in his mind, he remembered lyrics from a punk band that David loved and would often quote: *"Just remember God is faithful, even if you don't have faith yourself."*

These words were a comfort and a challenge to Nick as he mourned the loss of his brother. How could he remember God was faithful even now, when this had happened? As his own faith wavered, he asked God to help him where he did not have the faith himself. He was encouraged to know that it was not about him having the faith, but about remembering God is faithful.

A couple of weeks after the funeral, Nick took some flowers to a run down street that was on the route he regularly took between my house and his. Behind a wall was a patch of dirt without any signs of life or growth.

If he had been in Melbourne, he would have left flowers at the police station, but trying to find a way to grieve David's loss, he laid the flowers here instead.

"Every year more than 800,000 people take their own life and there are many more people who attempt suicide. Suicide occurs throughout the lifespan and was the second leading cause of death among 15–29-year-olds globally in 2012." (World

Health Organisation, http://www.who.int/mental_health/prevention/suicide/ suicideprevent/en/)

What causes someone so young to decide that there is no other way out of the pain they feel but to end it all?

Through the work of Pure, my team and I regularly meet and mentor young people who have attempted to take their own lives or struggled with suicidal thoughts. This question is something we grapple with regularly. When we started Courageous, a mentoring program for boys, it was an issue that came up time and time again. Dr Elikem Tamaklo, our course founder, writes this about a lad he met on the course:

"Seated towards the back and chatting with his mates, Jack exuded an air of confidence that highlighted him from the group.

We had just started our second pilot of the Courageous course with great fanfare and excitement – and this group of lads were very happy to be out of class.

During the group sessions, Jack could always be counted on to say the right thing in contrast with his mates. He was kind, conscientious, loved football and seemed like he had everything in order. He seemed ... 'normal'. However, in the one-on-one sessions, as weeks rolled by, he began to open up about his life and we began to realise it was very far from the idyllic picture he portrayed. Behind the façade, Jack was struggling.

His father died when he was a child and he lived with his Mum and her current boyfriend, the latest in a long string of men. After our session on dealing with anger I spent some time chatting to him. Pushing back the tears that were welling up in his eyes, he told me of how he felt angry most of the time and he didn't know why. He told me of how he tried very hard to keep in control and do good, but there were times when he couldn't keep his emotions in. Waves of anger would roll out, resulting in callous words and actions he regretted later.

He told me that the week before his Mum had falsely accused him of neglecting his chores. He had been so angry with her that in an instant, he reached out and grabbed her throat. At this point, the walls holding his tears back disintegrated, releasing cascading streams of guilt and shame as he narrated his horror at realising what he had done.

'I can't believe I did that ... I was so angry that I couldn't control myself ... I feel so bad ... I just want to die...'

The extent of his struggle had been so overwhelming that at the time that he had thought of killing himself. My heart broke as I saw a boy, desperately trying to overcome the feelings of guilt and shame that had kept him from mentioning this to anyone else.

I told him of my own struggles as a boy navigating life to becoming a man. I told him of my mistakes and my victories. I told him that I saw in him a boy who had enormous potential to overcome life's challenges and thrive. I told him of how I believed he had been created with purpose and strength and how I would stand by him as he overcame this particular challenge. We connected with the school's child-safeguarding officer and the pastoral team and together, supported Jack as he began to deal with his feelings in a real and meaningful way.

My heart swelled at our last Courageous session as Jack approached me. With a smile and heartfelt gratitude he told me of how much the last few weeks had meant to him and ended with two more powerful words: 'Thank you'."

I have found it so encouraging that we have been able to support young people like Jack. It reminds me that there is something we can do to help young people – like David – who are struggling with the anger they feel. There is a way to see the course of their life change.

I tried my best to support Nick as he navigated through the grief and pain he felt. It was a confusing and difficult time, and dealing with the loss of his brother wasn't the only challenge he faced in the first year of being in Liverpool.

14

WALKING IN THE DARK

When Nick arrived in Liverpool the only job he could find was in a nursing home, where he worked from 7am until 2pm each day. Every shift he washed and dressed the elderly patients and turned those who were bedridden over onto their sides so they wouldn't get bedsores. His role also included helping each elderly person go to the toilet and wiping their bottom. Nick dealt with patients with scabies, dementia and gangrenous wounds. There were times where he would nearly vomit from the smell.

On one occasion he was called in to turn a woman who was about to die. This lady was covered in open sores and suffering from the flesh eating bug MRSA. A professional nurse with years of experience had been called in to attend to her, but she began vomiting over and over due to the repugnant smell. As a last resort Nick was called in and he lovingly turned this elderly lady over one last time, to try and make her more comfortable in her last hours.

Was this the future God had promised? Was this really where we were both meant to be? If God had a plan for us, shouldn't it have been easier?

Then a job to work with inner city youth came up and it looked perfect for Nick. It seemed at last that things were changing and this endless grey season was nearly over. Nick went for the interview excited, finally feeling that God was showing him the reason he was in Liverpool. But Nick didn't get the job. A friend of ours was offered it instead. Nick had hoped this job would be the beginning of something great for him, but instead he was launched back into the wilderness. It seemed as though God was playing a cruel trick. Why would He open up this seemingly perfect opportunity for Nick, taunt him with it, then whisk it away and give it to someone else?

For Nick, most days were a struggle and there seemed to be no way out. But still each day he pressed into God.

As Nick and I prayed together during these grey days, we were reminded of the life of Moses. We were encouraged to remember that Moses' journey was not straightforward. Even though he had been rescued as a baby and had grown up as royalty, he had ended up in the wilderness. We talked about the shock it must have been for Moses to suddenly go from living in a palace to living with nomads in the desert. The Bible tells us that Moses spent forty years there, herding sheep, before God appeared to him in a burning bush and called him to lead the Israelites out of slavery.

His life had started off with so much promise. He had grown up as a prince. There had even been a time when he thought he could do something to free his own people from slavery. Now he was just a shepherd in the desert and he probably thought nothing was ever going to change. Yet, God had purpose in the wilderness time for Moses. In this place he was given space to grow and develop character.

We thought everything would fall into place when Nick got his visa to come back to the UK. It seemed like we'd finally got the breakthrough we were praying for. Instead, Nick entered one of the longest wilderness times he had ever experienced – placed in an unknown city with a lack of purpose, a difficult job and, hardest of all, grieving the death of David.

In every painful season we have a choice. Will we let it defeat us, crush us, cut us out of the game? Or will we walk through it, trusting God and allowing Him to help us grow through the pain of our wilderness? In the wilderness it can feel like God has deserted us. Sometimes in this place it seems that trying to connect with God is almost impossible. Still, God is there even if we can't feel, hear or see Him.

"Even when I walk through the darkest valley, I will not be afraid, for you are close beside me. Your rod and your staff protect and comfort me." (Psalm 23:4 NIV)

Over and over again the Bible promises us that even when we walk through the darkest times in life, God remains close beside us. Like a shepherd guarding His sheep, He watches over us. God does not disappear when life gets tough. He is there to be sought by us more than ever.

From our limited perspective, the youth work job had seemed like the perfect opportunity for Nick, but in reality the friend who got it found it really difficult. The job involved living far away from our church community and meant attending a different church. With hindsight we realised it would actually have been the worse thing for Nick at the time and we could see that God was working for our good

"And we know that God causes everything to work together for the good of those who love God and are called according to his purpose for them." (Romans 8:28 NLT)

Life is not always clear-cut and by no means is this verse meant to be used as a sticking plaster that neatly covers a gash and hides the pain beneath it. The apostle Paul, the person who wrote this, knew what it was to suffer. He knew the pain of betrayal, loss and persecution. Yet through all his trials he writes that God works these things together for the good in the lives of those who love Him. It is in the midst of pain that this is true, but it takes faith to realise it. God is good and Scripture tells us that He is always working for our good in every situation.

As the months went on, Nick was accepted onto a course at

university, something that he had never thought was possible due to the fact he would have to pay such high fees as an international student. Around the same time he was also given a job running children's and youth satellite churches called Kids Klub, which provided an income for him. Nick ran these Kids Klubs in some of the poorest areas in Liverpool. He met young people whose brothers had been shot or whose parents worked in dead end jobs and found that his own struggles in the past year meant he was more able to understand some of the struggles they were facing.

Little by little he could see that God's hand had been on his life, even in the times when Nick was nearly certain God was no longer there. God did, in fact, have purpose to use all the pain he had walked through. As he recounted all of this, those lyrics David had loved trailed through his mind again:

"Just remember God is faithful, even when you don't have faith yourself."

15

OVERCOMING

"I'm not going to school," I screamed, "You can't make me!"

* * *

Picture a grey Monday morning, obligatory school run time. The car engine running while our next door neighbour, Susan, tries to help my Mum coax me into the car. The more she tries, the more hysterical I become until eventually, with a look of concern, she takes my brother by the hand and gives him a lift to school instead. My Mum is left to deal with me...

My brother had it tough that year. I was his older sister, who in earlier years had been the one making up games and cheerfully bossing him around. Yet now I couldn't even get into a car to go to school. I was eleven years old and hemmed in by fear.

How did I get here?

No one could have controlled the circumstances that had led to this point. It was unclear then, but now as I trace the story back I see how small thoughts rooted themselves deep into my young mind until their grip was so tight I could hardly move. First, my godmother was diagnosed with cancer. With short notice and little explanation my Mum was whisked away to help look after her. Then, at school a short while later, the secretary came into our classroom to inform my friend that her parents had been in a car accident. Our teacher did very little to soothe the situation while tears streamed down my friend's face as she was taken away by the secretary. As I watched her leave, that unassuming little question planted itself in my mind: *what would happen if my Mum died?*

I didn't forget about it at lunchtime. It hovered over my mind the rest of the afternoon and, by that evening, it was a shadow that I could not shake. What would happen if she wasn't there any more? My Mum ran our household; she was the one who made it a light and happy place. She cooked the meals, she made the house look beautiful, and she supported my hard working Dad. When she wasn't there, our home felt like a very different place. What would happen if she never came home?

As these thoughts churned over and over inside of me, fear began to cloud my vision. There seemed to me only one option to ensure we did not lose her. Somewhere deep inside my childish mind I resolved not to leave her side. I didn't go to school for three months. They tried to talk it through with me, reasoned with me, pleaded, bribed, joked and cried, but the door of my mind was bolted shut and nothing could penetrate it.

This fear, which had started small, had taken control of my life and it was affecting my entire family. My Mum and Dad were deeply distressed by this situation and were under pressure. Legally, the facts were that they could be taken to court and sentenced to up to three months in prison if I didn't start going back to school soon.

For some reason school had become the place I feared more than most. The whole place felt bleak and pointless. Even the idea of going filled me with dread and each time someone new tried to persuade me to go, I'd shut down until they gave up and left me alone.

I knew what I was feeling wasn't right. I knew that I should be going to school like my brother, like everybody else. Still something within me refused to be persuaded.

"What is wrong with me? Why can't I be normal and go like everyone else? Am I going to be like this forever? They don't get it, they don't understand what I am feeling. They can't help me. No one understands me...".

In my mind, the silent questions rolled on and on. Desperation built up inside of me until I felt that suicide was the only way out and I tried to strangle myself with my dressing gown cord. It would never have worked, but I didn't know that at the time.

The school welfare officer, our doctor, the head teacher and a therapist all tried to work out how to help me. They tried to "solve" the problem and get me back into full time education.

The whole family were obliged to attend family therapy sessions in an effort to find a way through the situation. My brother sat obediently on his chair while I refused to cooperate. Instead, I hid behind the sofa, eating strawberry laces, and tried to coax him into joining my rebellion.

It felt utterly hopeless until I met Jackie. She was different. She spent her time getting to know me before she asked anything of me or even brought up the subject of my absence at school. Days turned into weeks as she came round to talk to me about the latest episode of *Neighbours*, chatted to me about the characters and took in interest in who I was as a person.

The people who had tried to help me before were nice enough, but I knew their interest in me ended when the allotted time was up. The time they spent with me was focused clearly on trying to find a way to slot me nicely back into the education system. With Jackie it was different, she seemed to be genuinely interested in who I was. I saw her as my ally, someone who really wanted to help me. I wasn't just another statistic of school phobia to her. I was a person in my own right with my own identity and worth.

Because she had got to know me, I listened to what she had to say when the topic of my school attendance did come up. She had come up with a plan, tailor made for me, and I trusted her enough to try it.

That first day back at school was full of tears. In fact, most of the weeks following it were full of tears too. I became well known by my peers for crying in class, but I persevered and eventually learnt that I could "feel the fear and do it anyway".

Each time I pushed through the fear and all the what-if's that swirled around my mind, I won another small battle in the war. Fear was my foe in this war and each battle gave me increased strength for the next one. This wasn't just going to go away after one breakthrough.

The only way to overcome any addiction or fear is step by step. Each little victory gives us strength for the next fight, until one day we find we've won the war completely.

My thinking needed to be changed and this took discipline.

As I grew up, this fear remained with me. At every key event in my life that involved a new step outside my comfort zone, fear would present itself and I would have to face it head on. At school I had learnt to push through it, but I wasn't free from it yet. It wasn't until ten years later that I found greater freedom.

16

LETTING GO OF FEAR

Arriving in Liverpool had brought a whole new assortment of fears into my life, each one glinting as it was exposed. From the first day in this new city they began to cast their shadows over me. I had managed my fears before and continued to try and push through as I had been taught many years ago, but now it was time to discover the full freedom that Jesus had paid for me on the cross. Fear didn't need to lead my life any more. A new freedom was waiting.

Up until now, I had been managing my fears in the same way that I learnt as a child. It wasn't until I met Bel that I started to realise that God wanted me to be free from this fear. Instead of just battling with the same things over and over, God wants us to share our struggles and learn from others with more wisdom. When we open up to them, they're able to challenge the way we think and push us closer to God.

"And the things you have heard me say in the presence of many witnesses, entrust to reliable people who will also be qualified to teach others." (2 Timothy 2:2 NIV)

I met Bel at my church while studying at LIPA. I noticed her passion for God almost immediately and I could tell that I would learn a lot by spending time with her. As it turned out, 2 Timothy 2:2 was one of her favourite verses! As Bel and I spent time together she began to challenge the fear that I still lived with.

If being a disciple is really going to work, we have to be willing to be real, to be fully honest about our thoughts and lifestyle. Sometimes people miss out on this type of input because they're scared of being too vulnerable with someone else. Yet when I let her in, Bel helped me to see that this fear I struggled with had taken a huge and illegitimate place in my life. Fear had dominated my thinking to the point where it influenced who I thought God was.

"Don't copy the behaviour and customs of this world, but let God transform you into a new person by changing the way you think. Then you will learn to know God's will for you, which is good and pleasing and perfect." (Romans 12:2 NLT)

Bel gently showed me how to change the way I was thinking. She showed me what the Bible had to say about fear and helped me to practically apply this to my life until it made a real change. It didn't happen overnight, but her consistent and weekly investment in my life was powerful. Bit by bit she helped me form new patterns in my thinking until fear no longer controlled me.

I was finally free, but this still wasn't the end of my dealings with fear. When God sets us free from something it's life changing. But the next challenge is learning how to stay free. It's a bit like if I decided to start going to the gym to get fit. Once I've put in months of work to get in shape, I can't just stop going and expect my fitness levels to stay the same. If I don't stay disciplined and keep on going to the gym, I'm going to lose my fitness.

In same way, when we've found freedom from life controlling issues, we need to be disciplined enough to keep that freedom. For me this means I need to watch what I'm thinking about. God has given me a great imagination. It's a gift and part of where my ability to dream and have vision lies. But this imagination also means I can easily start imagining negative outcomes and begin to fear the worst. I've had to learn make this verse in 2

Corinthians a practice in my life, not just for a few months, but all time.

"Pulling down strongholds; casting down imaginations, bringing into captivity every thought and making it obedient to Christ." (2 Corinthians 10:4-5 NIV)

Imagine a runway at an airport where planes are landing constantly. At Heathrow airport in London planes land on each runway on average every 90 seconds (source: National Science Foundation). Now think about your mind as that runway. Every thought is like a plane coming in to land. According to research, the average person has as many as 50,000 thoughts each day (source: Answers.com). This works out as 35 thoughts each minute.

Imagine 35 planes landing on an airstrip each minute. It seems almost impossible to think that we can decide which thoughts land and which we turn away, but the Bible says we can:

"We take captive every thought and make it obedient to Christ." (2 Corinthians 10:5 NIV)

If we make a choice daily to stop certain thoughts from landing, we slowly begin to train our minds. For me this has literally meant that at times I have had to say "No" out loud and shake my head each time a thought came into mind that wasn't in line with God's word. The more I did this, the more of a fool I looked, so my mind caught on and began to stop those thoughts without me even realising it.

The same research goes on to say that 95% of these 50,000 thoughts are repeated daily. We think the same things over and over again, and those thoughts shape what we believe, how we speak and how we live (source: www.mind-sets.com). If the thoughts that are stuck "on repeat" in our mind are negative or not true, then it's no wonder we find ourselves trapped by them.

The way we think decides how we act. If we have a mindset that is fearful, then we'll probably be too scared to take a risk when God asks us to. If we're always thinking that we're not good enough, we're probably less likely to try something new. The discipline of training our minds to stop thoughts like this from landing is a biblical principle that helps us to find the freedom that is ready and waiting for us.

For me it has been a hard discipline to learn and one I continually need to revisit, especially when I'm travelling by plane.

I've never been a big fan of flying. Once, just before I was due to take a trip to Australia, there were a number of stories in the newspapers about missing flights and planes which had been shot down. I read every one of them, which for me was probably not the best idea.

The words I read set in me an increased nervousness as our flights approached. During turbulence, my heart began to beat faster and my palms started to sweat. My imagination took over and there were times during that flight when my whole body shook with fear. With the newspaper headlines fresh in my memory every possibility raced through my mind. It was a real wake up call. I had let my mind become undisciplined, forgetting what reading those newspaper articles could trigger in me.

So what did I do? Did I decide I would never fly again? Did I opt out? Of course not! I wanted to do that, but instead I chose to focus on God. For me this meant that when the fear arose as I flew, I listened to worship music and prayed, speaking out Scripture, while beginning to say "no" and shake my head each time a thought tried to enter my mind. This was the process needed to stop my mind from going down that path of imagining the worst. I would even go into the plane bathroom, jump around and speak the word of God over myself and ask God to fill me afresh with His Spirit.

The truth is, each time we refuse a thought, we reinforce our determination to prevent it accessing the landing strip of our mind. With every aborted landing our mind becomes stronger and as a result, the negative thoughts begin to come less and less.

There is a battle for our minds. We do have an enemy and he wants us to get stuck in the sticky substance of fear. But, more importantly, we have an awesome, powerful, perfect God who is with us and has given us victory and authority in every situation. Therefore we need to be disciplined and take hold of that God-given authority. Remembering who God is and what He can do is so important, because our lives are held in His hands.

"There is none like God, who rides across the skies to rescue you." (paraphrase of Deuteronomy 33:26)

This discipline applies in so many different areas of our lives. Whether it is an issue of comparison, self-hatred, suicidal thoughts or something else – we have authority through Jesus to not allow those thoughts to land. It takes discipline, it is hard work, but it is so crucial.

Each one of us can ask someone who we want to learn from to disciple us and each of us can be open and willing to teach and pass on what we have learnt to another. As we do this we will see those around us, who are trapped, beginning to walk in freedom and in the knowledge of who they are in Christ.

Back when Nick and I were on Activate, someone in our team felt God had showed them a picture for Nick. It was of a beautiful engagement ring, full of promise, but it was buried in maggots. To get to the ring involved putting your hand in among the maggots and pulling it out. Sometimes life can be like this. There are good things waiting for us, amazing promises that God has given us, but it feels like we have to put our hand into the maggots to reach them. Nick and I both faced different challenges in our first year together in Liverpool and sometimes it felt like we were just grasping at maggots. But when I began to discover God's life changing truth, it made all the difference. The fear that had trapped me didn't have the same power any more. I had found freedom and God was using all I had learnt through this process for His purposes.

17

AWAKENING

A thin mist covered the ground from about ten inches up. Unusual, but it was to signify a glorious day. Soon the mist cleared and the sun broke through, boasting bright blue sky all around it. It was midsummer day and what a display for the middle of summer. The girl awoke, eyes blurry, taking several minutes to become accustomed to the light.

The boy had been awake for hours. He had woken with nervous energy. Heart pumping in his chest, he crept out of the house. Taking his bike, he quickly pedalled his way through the mist, feeling its cold, damp effect on his neck.

"White roses, a bouquet please," he asked the florist. She handed them to him and he continued on, led by the scent of freshly baked goods from the local bakery. Here he purchased two *pain au chocolat*, the girl's favourite.

He arrived back at the house where the girl slept again without stirring and on a piece of cream paper he wrote the words:

"I Love you Beautiful."

Taking the white roses, *pain au chocolat* and freshly brewed coffee, he made his way to the girl's room. Today was the day. The maggots had dispersed and he had found the ring. The girl heard a knock at the door.

"Come in."

In came the boy with his hands full. The girl beamed as she read the note. She breathed in the sweet scent of the roses and said thank you as she took a good gulp of coffee.

A little while later they left the house. Hand in hand, they made their way to the riverbank, chatting and laughing as they walked. Down the hill, through the alleyway made of bowing trees, until they reached the river Ouse, where boaters pottered slowly without a care in the world.

The boy talked of his hopes for the future and the girl listened intently. The girl talked of the life less ordinary she desired and together they dreamt about the God-adventures they could have.

Further down the riverbank they came to some little red boats. The girl smiled; red was her favourite colour. The boy had hired one and soon they were aboard.

The boy navigated the boat, talking about his father's motor boat that he had grown up with. The girl was used to sailing boats. Further and further they went, until they reached a sewage works. The boy exclaimed hotly and they turned around. That had obviously not been the plan!

Later, in a more appropriately scented spot, the boy got down on one knee, tears in his eyes, and spoke about how much the girl meant to him.

"Will you marry me?" he asked, as he pulled a small blue box from his pocket.

At this very moment, the boat plunged into the bank and both boy and girl fell to the floor laughing.

"Yes," she cried, "I will!"

The boy slid the ring onto the fourth finger of her left hand, where it would stay for the rest of her life.

Wake up...!

The girl pinched herself. Was this a dream?

Life is not a fairy tale, but there are some days which feel so wonderful they could surely only happen in our dreams. This day was real. The season of maggots had been a tough one, but like the word said, an engagement ring waited. We had found it, and now it was on my finger!

The train journey back to Liverpool had always filled me with a sense of dread, but this time as we travelled back from York to share our exciting news it seemed that everything was about to change. And it did – in more ways than I expected.

The year ahead was already mapped out. It was my final year of university. I was planning to live with Clare and Sam in the same house where I'd lived for the past two years. The arrangement was okay. I hated the house, but Clare was my closest friend from university which made it better. However, what happened next meant that all my plans had to change. It seemed like a disaster at first and meant that September began with a bump.

Over the summer Clare had had some issues with our landlord. Then, the week I arrived back at our house, he had told us he was selling it and we had to leave immediately. Panic and indignation rose in our throats. We were all going to be homeless. Could he do this to us? It was not a great start to our final year at university and, what's more, Nick and I had a wedding to plan!

As I began to think about different places I could live, I decided to phone Jenny Harding, one of the pastors of our church. Jen and her husband Nic often had lodgers in their home and I wondered if perhaps they might have a room for me. I explained the situation to her and sheepishly asked if there might be space in their home for another lodger. To my surprise, without missing a beat Jen replied, "Nic and I would love you to live with us. Our only condition would be that we like who you are engaged to and we love Nick, so come and live with us."

A few days later I moved into Nic and Jen's home. It was the best thing that could have happened to me. I immediately felt welcome in their home – a beautiful three-storey house filled with love, laughter and the smell of Jen's incredible cooking. On the top floor Anna and Debbie were lodging in rooms either side of me, two amazing women who would soon become some of my best friends.

What a change. In one week I had gone from homeless to living in the dream house. A warm family atmosphere, a floor with friends in rooms either side of me and a big family dinner each night where Jen would cook and we ate like kings. Living here transformed the way I felt about Liverpool. I fell in love with Nic and Jen, their heart for the city and the community they created around them. Seeing their integrity at home, as well as the way they led their church, created a connection with my church, Frontline, which I hadn't had before.

Around this time I was also given opportunities to start serving in the church by singing in the worship team and leading a small group. I had a part time job working in a restaurant, was learning to drive and Nick and I were planning our wedding. On top of all of this I was in my final year at university, writing my dissertation and, as part of my course, setting up a pilot theatre company called Elevate at another performing arts college. Life was full, but I was fully awake and thriving.

Over the years God had been planting a desire in my heart to somehow help young people discover who God has created them to be and see them released into that potential. I had come to LIPA because I felt God calling me to use my passion for performing to do this. I didn't have it all planned out but now, in my final year at university, all I had learnt was being weaved, formed and spun together. This dream was in the process of becoming a reality as flesh and tendons brought together the bones of the ideas that had been waiting to come to life. This dream was called Pure. It began to be something I prayed about regularly and then actively pursue.

The dream is a golden sea of faces, golden because they reflect HIM. His light.

I saw this vision during this year while praying with a group of women – a dream of all those God was calling us to impact and see come alive in Him. As I glimpsed their faces, I saw each one who God was calling me to reach out to – the thousands in the valley of decision – and my heart broke. I knew that I wanted to give all I had to reach out to them.

For me, the whole of my time at LIPA was about seeing this dream realised and now the secrets of my heart were to be brought to life. God had used my first two years in Liverpool as a time of discipleship and preparation, but this year was about awakening. Tendons, muscle and flesh began to cover each bone of vision until, it was time to step out.

18

GLIMPSES

"I'm a lap dancer," one of the girls blurted out. She was a student from the Theatre in Education module I was teaching at Liverpool College. "It really helps my confidence and self-esteem."

"Does it really?" I questioned, wondering if she really believed the words that she was saying.

"I'm cutting myself," another confided. "It helps me feel something, rather than just being numb."

It was like someone had pulled out the stopper and all these secrets were bubbling over, pouring out of their mouths onto anyone who would listen. It just so happened that this anyone was me.

My university lecturer had done a deal with his friend, a lecturer at the local community college, so that I could teach a class in Theatre in Education at Liverpool College. In return, these unsuspecting students became the performers I needed for my pilot theatre company, Elevate, which was to tour schools in Liverpool with a performance about peer pressure.

They were an unlikely mix and from the start I could see that they were struggling with many of the issues I wanted to address in the performance. I began to work with this group to look at ways we could develop a piece of theatre that would engage and impact a group of school pupils. To bring this to life we looked at their own stories, until some of these became blended into the piece they would perform.

It was a tough process, with moments of break down and even hysteria. One girl dropped out because she was still struggling with the issues we were addressing and it became too upsetting for her to be part of the performance. But after a lot of hard work, and many days where I doubted we would ever get there, we finally had a wonderful piece of theatre that was ready to perform. I sent out letters to schools across the city telling them about the performance and before I knew it, my lecturer handed me a pile of letters from schools literally lining up to book us. I was astounded!

At the end of our first booking a drama teacher came up to me with tears streaming down her face. During the workshop that we ran about peer pressure after the performance, one of her pupils finally admitted that she was being bullied. The teacher had known this for a while, but had never been able to get the girl to speak to her about it. Through the use of theatre, and God working through it, this girl had opened up for the first time.

The success of this project only fuelled my passion to do this work more. It had been a hard process, but I was so excited about what I had seen happen through the Elevate tour. If God could do that through a group of college students who didn't know Him yet, what could He do through a group who were passionate to see God impact schools? The possibilities were limitless!

I began to seek God about the next steps for this vision I had for Pure, praying and asking Him to lead me. I talked a lot to a friend from Activate days, Kyra, who had a similar heart for young people. Together we dreamed of what God could do. I began to plan how I could set up a theatre company and looked at what qualifications I'd need. There was no way I could run a theatre company fresh out of university. At the age of 22, surely I was too young to take such a risk? Instead, I started looking at other options. I found a great PGCE course at Warwick University and decided I'd train as a Drama teacher first. I would work in a school for a while and then, once I had more experience, think about setting up Pure.

One night God powerfully spoke to me in the most surprising way while I was stewarding at a local youth event. There was so much on my heart about Pure that night, as I stood among the young people and watched the bands play, and I began to pray for those around me.

Suddenly, a man I had never met before tapped me on the shoulder and began to share what he felt God saying to him about me. I stood amazed as he spoke so specifically about the things that had been on my mind and the fears that I was fighting with. He wrote some of it down on the back of a popcorn box that I still have:

"Be prepared to be called into a radically more active ministry concerning a very specific area of life ministry. If you are obedient to Him when He calls you, He will bless you very specifically in your life. This is not a temporary thing, I believe you're called to intercede into specific situations, possibly to young women who know their mums but not their mum's love, which must mean you've got coach loads of love to give to young sisters and daughters.

Don't worry, He'll enable you in your weakness. In your inability, His strength will show through. Please remember, it's not your strength. The secret is in your dependence on your God. The sacrifice will be become a massive bonus, life changing, so that others won't just notice, but will be affected by the anointing resting on you."

This was such an incredible word of encouragement to me. It spoke right into the vision of Pure and what I was sensing God was saying.

I spent a lot of my time during that year praying. My room in Nic and Jen's house was set up like a 24-7 prayer room, with scriptures on the walls, space to write, read the Bible and hear from God and this word only fuelled my prayer times more.

No dream that God gives can come into existence without prayer. Prayer is the key to seeing something come out of nothing and prayer was the centre point of this entire year. In my room on that top floor, I would pray and seek the Lord about this vision that He had placed in my heart.

"The earnest prayer of a righteous person has great power and produces wonderful results. Elijah was as human as we are, and yet when he prayed earnestly that no rain would fall, none fell for three and a half years! Then, when he prayed again, the sky sent down rain and the earth began to yield its crops." (James 5:16-18 NLT)

As I prayed, God spoke and things began to happen bit by bit.

One of my favourite examples of the power of prayer can be found in 1 Kings 18. There are some key lessons we can learn from this passage, which applied to me as I was in this stage of birthing a new ministry. Even if I didn't realise that's what I was doing at the time.

Early on in the story, Elijah the prophet tells King Ahab that there's going to be a drought. Then after three and a half years with no rain, Elijah brings another message to the king. This time, he tells him to get ready, because there's a storm coming. Every time I read this I'm always so amazed at Elijah's confidence. He has complete faith that God can do what He promised.

"Then Elijah said to Ahab, 'Go get something to eat and drink, for I hear a mighty rainstorm coming!' So Ahab went to eat and drink. But Elijah climbed to the top of Mount Carmel and bowed low to the ground and prayed with his face between his knees. Then he said to his servant, 'Go and look out toward the sea.'

The servant went and looked, then returned to Elijah and said, 'I didn't see anything.' Seven times Elijah told him to go and look. Finally the seventh time, his servant told him, 'I saw a little cloud about the size of a man's hand rising from the sea.' Then Elijah shouted, 'Hurry to Ahab and tell him, "Climb into your chariot and go back home. If you don't hurry, the rain will stop you!" And soon the sky was black with clouds. A heavy wind brought a terrific rainstorm." (1 Kings 18:41-45 NLT)

Elijah's job doesn't end once he's told Ahab that the rain is coming. He knows that he still has an active part to play in seeing the rain come. Once Ahab leaves, he climbs up a mountain and begins to pray with his head between his knees, as if he's in labour and about to give birth. He doesn't stop praying until he is told the rain cloud is there and then Elijah acts.

It was clear that God was speaking to me about setting up Pure. The dream had been growing in my heart since I was a young teenager praying in my youth group, and in school sitting alongside Leila while she struggled with anorexia. It had been tried out a little and now, like Elijah, it was the time to pray in faith.

Zoe and John were friends of ours who were also engaged and looking for a place to live once they got married. As they prayed about where to live, God told them clearly that they were going to move into a flat above a shop. We would often drive past it and Zoe would speak out what God had told them: this flat was theirs, it would belong to them.

The flat was not for sale. Nor was there any sign it would be. But God had spoken so clearly and so Zoe was obedient to pray and speak out in faith that this promise would come to pass. Then one day, the flat suddenly came on the market. They put in an offer and it was accepted.

At the time, this was such an encouragement to me. An amazing illustration of how God so often works. He sows a seed, a promise in our hearts of what could be, and then He asks as to work with Him and pray and declare in faith until the promise is fulfilled. So often the seeds are sown, but we neglect to water and nurture the seeds with prayer.

In this year God showed me time and time again illustrations of the vital part that prayer plays in seeing His promises come to fruition. But prayer is more than just a way God works with us to make things happen. When we pray, we are spending time with God and the more we time we spend with Him, the more we get to know Him. In prayer, God shapes us and shows us a different perspective. He gives us ideas and strategies for situations that only He could come up with. Even when we don't know how to pray, as we try, He teaches us. The important thing is to try! The more we pray the more we learn to pray. As we spend time with Him, we find He has all we need to accomplish the work He has given us to do.

It's so easy to get swept up by the busyness of life and begin thinking that we don't have time to pray. But the reality is, prayer is the most important thing we can do. Prayer is the fuel that launches us into the air, as we step out into what we are made for.

Section 3
FIRST STEPS

It is easy for a baby bird to become comfortable in the familiar setting of its nest. Sometimes, parent birds need to push the baby out in order to get it to fly. If they are to survive, they must learn to fly, and unless they learn to flap their wings, they will keep hitting the ground. Even when the bird has experienced flight for the first time, it still takes practice to step out and flap its wings to their fullest potential.

19

HAVE I GOT WHAT IT TAKES?

Fast forward to 2009. My blood pressure was high; I had just been diagnosed with gestational diabetes and it was a month until I was due to give birth to our first son. In the early hours of Sunday morning I was woken by what I thought were Braxton Hicks, "practice" contractions. I tried to go back to sleep as there was a busy day ahead of us, where Nick and I were both speaking at different church services. The next day the Braxton Hicks returned. We were about to move house and had a lot to do before the baby arrived, so I just tried to continue with the day. Throughout the day we kept bumping into older friends who confidently told us it would be ages until we had the baby.

"First babies are always late," they said. Then, after another busy day, I collapsed into bed and my waters broke. We rushed into hospital and I realised that the contractions I'd been having weren't practice ones, they were the real thing!

Eventually, we were taken into a room where I was examined and told that I was ready to start pushing, but it wasn't that straightforward. Our baby boy's heartbeat had slowed down. The umbilical cord was wrapped around his neck and this meant oxygen was not getting through to his heart. What started as a normal examination became an emergency situation. He needed to be delivered straight away. A blur followed. Needles were poked into me, doctors roughly examined me and forms of consent were waved in front of me to sign. The words "paralysis" and "headaches" swam around my head as I tried to make sense of the form in front of me and what I was signing away. Before I knew it, I was in theatre. A needle was jabbed in my back for the spinal anaesthetic and I asked a nurse, "Am I going to die now?"

"No..." she replied, but she didn't fill me with much confidence.

Using forceps, they pulled our son out and rushed him away to make sure he was okay. Thankfully, he was. I however, was not. A few hours later I began to lose a lot of blood and as midwives and doctors surrounded me, fear crept up on me. "Can I really do this? Can I be a mother to this little one? Do I have what it takes?"

At the start of every new challenge, I've always had this nagging question deep down inside of me. *Do I have what it takes to make this happen?*

The blank sheet of paper in front of me at the beginning of an essay. The search for words to perform when auditioning for parts I really wanted. Each time this surge of uncertainty would rise in me: *Am I good enough? Can I really do this?*

* * *

When I was about 16 I had this idea about running an event in York Minster, the big cathedral in my home town. Excitedly, I told my youth leader how I imagined it filled with people worshipping God and her offhand comment has always stuck with me:

"Tamsin, you have all these great ideas, but do you ever do anything?" She was right. Would I ever actually do anything?

From that point on, every time I started something new, doubt would creep into my mind. There were times on Activate where it would get the better of me. I'd be asked to share a testimony in front of a group of school pupils, then a few hours before, panic would set in and I would drop out. In these moments, fear made the decisions.

During my last year of university I was very cautious about who I shared the vision of Pure with. I had this sense that I needed to carefully nurture it, protecting it from people who might damage it with their, "I'll believe it when I see it" attitude while it was still forming in me.

But there were others, like Nic Harding, the pastor of my church, who were great encouragers. When I shared my idea to set up Pure with Nic, he believed in me and in the vision I had. Living with Nic and Jen meant that we would often chat about it and his encouragement provided a great environment for the dream to grow.

Some people, who I had expected to be encouraging, actually really criticised my vision for Pure. In the beginning this criticism would cause me to doubt that I really had heard from God and send me back down the path of thinking that Pure was just another idea that I wouldn't do anything about. But God used this criticism to teach me how to push through that question – *Have I got what it takes?* – and see the bigger picture. I also learnt that sometimes when people criticise you, it doesn't always mean they're against the vision. Sometimes they're just seeing a much bigger picture than you can see at that moment, like my friend Rich.

Nick and I were at the house of our friends, Cate and Rich's, for dinner one night when I nervously shared my dream to set up Pure with them. I hadn't told many people, but it had come up in conversation and Cate was one of my closest friends. The response I received from Rich completely shocked me:

"That is a terrible idea ... it's sexist! What about the guys? They have potential too you know!" He became quite angry about it and I didn't know how to respond. These were my friends. I wanted them to support me. Instead Rich spent ten minutes outlining the reasons why this vision, that I thought was from God, was completely wrong.

Was he right? Had I got it all wrong? If some of my closest friends thought it was a bad idea, what made me think that I could start something like this on my own?

A few weeks later Rich asked to meet with me and, to my surprise, he offered to manage Pure. I was stunned.

"But you think it's sexist," I said. "You don't agree that God would establish something just for girls and not boys."

He told me that God had spoken to him about helping me with it and he wanted to obey. Here's what I wrote in my diary the day after:

Tuesday 22nd May 2003
Yesterday Rich offered to manage Pure. He'd obviously been praying about it and it seems that God led him to offer this amazing service. He'd already worked out a budget and would work out all our funding and basically manage us. His input yesterday has enabled me to dream again. He said that he could see Jesus in this. "It will happen." When someone else puts their faith in something, it's so encouraging and so exciting. So now to seek Gods will in all of this...

It was such an encouragement for me to see how God changed Rich's mind about Pure. It reminded me that if God wanted this to happen, He was well able to change the minds of critics and bring the right people to work alongside me.

Rich was full of all kinds of entrepreneurial ideas about how to generate funds and grow Pure. One of the most memorable was the day he came to the rest of the team with a new strategy for our funding. We were excited to hear what he had to say and waited with baited breath to hear how Pure could become a sustainable charity and we might be able to draw a salary.

He started by talking about Pure merchandise and then homed in on "Pure underwear" – G-strings to be precise! He had even drawn a picture to illustrate it. The underwear would say "Pure" on the front to promote chastity and his first pitch to sell these items was to the pastor of a local Pentecostal church! We couldn't help but break into giggles at the very idea of Rich pitching "Pure G-strings" to a Pentecostal pastor in order to encourage chastity. Rich had some great ideas, but this one took things to another level we didn't want to explore. Instead we fell about laughing. Thankfully, he took it well and soon moved onto a new idea.

Initially, it felt like Rich was very critical of the vision I had for Pure. But, looking back, I realise that actually he was seeing something much bigger than I was able to at the time.

20

IMPOSSIBLE IS NOTHING

Do I have what it takes?

It's a question we all face before stepping out into something new. There's just one problem with this question. It centres on "I" and if we put the focus there, then we are in trouble. If God has called us to step out, then He will give us everything we need. It's not about you or me having what it takes. It's about Him.

In the Bible, time and time again, we see God use the most unlikely people. When God told Abraham in Genesis 15:5 that he would have as many descendants as the stars in the skies, he must have wondered, "Do I have what it takes?" His wife Sarah couldn't conceive and now they were both too old to make it humanly possible. I'm sure her question was the same.

But here's the problem: when Abraham and Sarah focused on the "I" and did the sums, they decided they didn't have what it took. So instead of waiting for God to give them the son He'd promised, they took things into their own hands. At Sarah's suggestion Abraham slept with her servant, Hagar, and Ishmael was born. This was not what God had promised and it caused a whole host of problems.

When we leave God out of the equation and focus only on what we can do, we come to the inevitable conclusion that, no, we don't have what it takes. But when we look to God, trusting that if He has called us He will give us all we need, then we'll see the miraculous happen – just like Abraham and Sarah did, when eventually they did have a son of their own (Genesis 21).

God is not confined by our ideas of what's possible. He's not concerned about our qualifications or what we think we can achieve. The whole of the Bible is full of unqualified men and women. When God called Moses, his response was that he was no orator (Exodus 4:10). He hated public speaking, yet God used him to lead the Israelites out of captivity. In Judges, Gideon is described as the weakest of his clan. He was timid, but God called him to lead an army. In the book of Joshua we hear about Rahab. She was a prostitute, yet God used her. Jacob was a liar (Genesis 27), yet God still blessed him. In the gospels we read about Mary. She was a teenager called to give birth to the Son of God! Peter was always putting his foot in it. He even lied about knowing Jesus, yet he's described as the rock that God built his Church upon (Matthew 16:18). Acts 8 tells us that Saul was a persecutor of Christians, yet God called him to a mighty future.

When God called each of these people, they had every reason to ask, "Do I have what it takes?" Still He used each of these men and women in mighty ways. He called them not because they were qualified, but because He knew that in their weakness they would have faith and trust in Him.

When the angel Gabriel came to Mary and told her that she was going to become pregnant with the Son of God, her response was this:

"How will this happen, since I am a virgin?" (Luke 1:34 NIV)

Fair question. This is her "Have I got what it takes?" moment. Yet the angel's response satisfies her:

"For nothing is impossible with God." (Luke 1:37 NIV)

I'm fairly certain I would have had a lot more questions about the logistics of the operation, doubts about whether I even wanted to be pregnant and the possibility of being a single mum. Her response always amazes me. She trusts what the angel has said and replies:

"I am the Lord's servant ... may everything you have said to me come true." (Luke 1:38 NLT)

What a response! One question about "how" and then she was satisfied with the answer. She believed what the angel said, even though she didn't understand it and was in no way qualified to see how it could happen. This needs to be our response when God calls us to step out and take a risk for Him. A faith-filled response, fuelled by the truth that nothing is impossible for God.

When we take the focus away from ourselves, we start to see the whole thing differently. It has never been about us, and it has always been about HIM.

Nobody expected David the shepherd boy, youngest of eight, to be chosen as king. Even Samuel, God's prophet, didn't see it coming. God had to remind Samuel that He does not look at outward appearances, but at the heart (1 Samuel 16:7) and what a heart David had. If you read the books of Samuel you'll see the phrase "David sought the Lord" used over and over again. David was determined to seek God's way and trust that He would make a way to deliver him.

Before he became king, there were many times when David could have taken matters into his own hands and killed Saul, the current king. King Saul was jealous of David and was trying to kill him, but David refused to behave in a similar way. Instead he completely trusted the promise that God made to him, believing that He would make it happen at the right time.

When God calls us, He has already given us all we need for our assignment. He's not looking for us to be strong or clever or have it all figured out. What He's looking for is our obedience and for us to trust Him.

There is a lot of freedom that comes from realising it is not about us being strong. When we finally begin to understand that God will make a way in our weakness, all the pressure to look like we've got it all figured out disappears. The apostle Paul takes it one step further in 2 Corinthians 11:30 when he says that if he has to boast about anything, he will boast only in his weakness. This is an interesting concept to outwork. What does it look like to boast in our weakness in daily life?

It's very tempting to try and present ourselves as completely perfect. But, honestly, most people don't want to meet another person who seems to have it all together. They love it when we are real and vulnerable, because it gives them permission to do the same. Sometimes when I'm in meetings with really influential people I find myself admitting that I often have no idea what I am doing. I've discovered that when I show my weakness like this, it takes the power of out "position" and others are free to open up and talk about the same feelings.

God works best in weakness. The bible says His strength is actually "perfected" in our weakness (2 Corinthians 12:9). It's liberating when we understand this and, as we share our weaknesses with others, we give them permission to do the same.

I have no qualifications in leadership or running an organisation, yet God has called me at this time to be the CEO of Pure Creative Arts. Do I have what it takes? Often the answer is no, and when I approach things in this light I'm freed up to boast in my weakness and trust God's strength to be perfected in me.

We can break the mould. We don't need to present a perfect version of ourselves when we know God's strength is made perfect in our weakness. Great hair, the latest fashion, success at work, these things are not wrong in themselves, but when we get caught up in trying to present a perfect image of ourselves to the world, we quickly forget that it's not about us.

Let's be people who are quick to share our weakness, trusting that if God wants us to step out into something new, He will provide for us and He will make the way.

Have you got what it takes? Probably not, but God has! And if you're asking this question, you are probably in the best place ever to step out on the adventure ahead with Him. Go on, I dare you!

21

STEPPING OUT

My heart was in my mouth, my palms sweating as I began to dial the number for the Liverpool Youth for Christ office.

I had been praying with a friend when she felt God say that I shouldn't wait until I was "qualified" before I started Pure, I should take a step of faith and start now. I wasn't sure. But I had nothing to lose so I told God that if this was from Him, I would push one door to see. If the door opened I would go through, if not then I would stick with my original plan to become a teacher first. It was time to step out. Leave the "what if's" and the "have I got what it takes?" behind and begin to act on what I'd heard God say.

Steve answered the phone and without pausing a stream of excited words fell from my mouth as I tried to explain the vision for Pure. Steve was encouraging and, seeing the potential in the vision I described, he offered to meet with me to talk about it further. At the end of the conversation he gave me the numbers of three more people I should contact.

"So the door hasn't closed then," I said out loud to myself as I stood in the hallway of Nic and Jen's house. I looked down at the barely legible scribbles I'd written on my notepad. One was a potential funder, another was a school's band in the north of Liverpool and the last was a Scripture Union contact who worked in schools. Feeling exhilarated from the rush of adrenaline that had come from making the first call, I was ready to keep going and call these new numbers.

I had asked God to only open the door if He wanted me to go through it. So far the door was wide open.

I called the potential funder first. Finance was one of my main concerns. Nick and I were about to get married and he was still a full time student. If I was going to set up Pure, we'd need some funding to make this happen. No one answered. Next, heart still pumping, I called the school's band in north Liverpool, called *Remedy*. Little did I know that the phone I was about to ring was in a recording studio and in that recording studio there was a group of people praying.

These people were part of the band and they worked for The Way Project. God had spoken to the leaders of Remedy and told them it was time to move to a different city. They had shared this news with the rest of the band and in that moment they were praying about the future. As they prayed, they began to sense that God was saying He would send someone with a new vision to take this work forward in a new way. In line with what they felt God was saying, they started to pray:

"Lord send us a visionary. Lord, make the phone ring."

And to their shock, right at that moment, it did.

Ring Ring, Ring Ring, Ring...

The sound broke into the prayer meeting and they looked at each other. Was this a distraction or an answer to prayer? Their leader picked up the phone.

"Hello, The Way Project."

My stomach turned over as I heard a man's voice answer. Fighting the fear that he would think I was crazy, I took Steve's advice and dived straight in to tell him about the vision for Pure: "Can I tell you about a vision I believe God has given me?" I asked.

A stunned silence followed and then Nathan, the man who answered, began to cry as he spoke on the other end of the phone. For a split second I wondered if actually he was the crazy one, not me. But as we talked it became more and more obvious that God was at work. God was doing something beyond anything we could understand and it was beginning to get really exciting.

The next day I took the train to Waterloo in the north of Liverpool to meet Nathan, his wife and another girl called Andrea who was part of Remedy. As we drank hot chocolate and got to know each other it became even more clear that God had connected us for a reason. We began to talk of our passion to share the gospel with young people and our heart to see each young person stand up for purity in their schools and not compromise on this. It was as though something just clicked into place. Straight away, Andrea knew that she wanted to be a part of Pure. The vision was exactly what was on her heart and she was in.

A few weeks later, Kyra, a friend I had known from my time with YFC, left her band Dependence in Newcastle and moved to Liverpool to join us in setting up Pure. The three of us began to pray together regularly, and as we did, God would open up opportunities for us.

We made contact with other organisations and had the opportunity to record the first song we wrote together called "Don't You Know." The church where Remedy had been based offered all kinds of help to see the vision realised. The recording studio that Remedy had been praying in was where we recorded our second, third and fourth songs. An office in that same church building became our first base and later we used the church space for theatre and dance rehearsals each Friday morning. That church still supports Pure today.

Through all of this, God kept on confirming that we were on the right track in astounding ways.

However, the basic reality of the situation was that if I was to set up Pure while Nick was still a student, we were going to need some financial support. As Nick and I prayed about it together, we felt God say that we needed to trust Him and obey. It wasn't always easy, but we knew that if God wanted each detail to come together He would make a way for it all to happen. We had to relax and trust Him with it all.

Several weeks before our wedding, we signed the lease on a flat that we felt God had spoken to us about, but still had no idea how we could afford to pay the rent.

Then, one weekend shortly before the wedding, we were in Edinburgh visiting one of my bridesmaids, Mimi.

On the Sunday morning we went with Mimi and her sister to their church. We arrived just before the service started and were seated near the back of the small hall. After the worship, the pastor of the church, began to speak. I don't remember exactly what she said until she suddenly stopped after about fifteen minutes of preaching, looked at Nick and said:

"You, stand up, God has something for you." Followed by a word to the congregation: "Church, pray in the Spirit for this man."

I was petrified and excited at the same time. What was happening? I tried to push the irrational thoughts out of my mind that she would prophesy that we shouldn't get married and tried to focus instead on what God was doing.

As the church prayed obediently, she pointed at me. "You stand up, God has something for you too. Are you together?"

We nodded, unsure what exactly "together" meant, but too mystified by the situation to ask. As we stood side by side, uncertain of what on earth to make of what was happening, but desperate to hear from God, we listened. This pastor began to prophesy. She had never met us before and she knew nothing about us. She couldn't even see us that clearly because we were at the back of the church. Yet she spoke with such clarity about specific things that were happening in our lives, that it was clear God was speaking to us through her.

She spoke about the call on Nick's life to lead and pastor, she spoke about the call on my life to work with girls and the ministry God had given me, even that it would be called Pure. She prophesied about our marriage, our wedding, and that we would have a house and a home, and a family.

We were amazed and encouraged by what she was saying, but the thing about this whole experience that was the most confounding was what followed.

She was telling us that we needed to know that God was calling us and that He would provide all we needed financially. So strongly was this impressed upon her that she wanted her church to play a part in demonstrating it.

She asked us to come to the front of the church and hold out our hands. Following this, she invited the congregation to pray and seek the Lord about how much money they might want to give to encourage us at this time.

We were then handed a basket and before we knew it the basket was overflowing with more money than it could hold, until they had to bring out a second basket. Embarrassed by the generosity of this church who had no idea who we were, yet bowled over by what God had done through this incredible, obedient pastor and congregation, we stood there sheepishly, unsure if we could accept such a gift.

What a demonstration of provision! We left the church amazed and encouraged that God knew us so intimately. He knew our worries, but He had called us and He illustrated His promise to provide for us.

When God calls us to take a step of faith for Him, He makes it clear which way to go. He doesn't leave us fumbling about in the dark. He is a good Father and He promises to direct our every step, but it's our job to step out and obey Him when He calls us.

Whenever we're in a place where it seems that God is calling us to take a step of faith for Him, but we're unsure, one of the best things to do is create some space in our lives to hear from Him. Practically this might mean cutting back on some of the things we do to create that space to hear God speak.

"He brought me out into a spacious place; he rescued me because he delighted in me." (Psalm 18:19 NIV)

God brings us out into open spaces so that He can speak to us and unlock the plans and purposes He has for us. In this space we can let go of our own plans, fears and things that would hold us back. If we fill our time with too many things, we neglect the space for God to speak into and potentially miss what He has to say to us.

There will always be a reason why "now" is not the right time. There were plenty of reasons why starting Pure straight out of university was not the right time. But God had spoken and as I took the first steps He confirmed to me that I was doing the right thing.

Jesus tells a story of people who are invited to a banquet. Each of them gets an invitation, but declines with an excuse as to why they cannot go.

"Jesus replied: 'A certain man was preparing a great banquet and invited many guests. At the time of the banquet he sent his servant to tell those who had been invited, "Come, for everything is now ready." But they all alike began to make excuses. The first said, "I have just bought a field, and I must go and see it. Please excuse me." Another said, "I have just bought five yoke of oxen, and I'm on my way to try them out. Please excuse me." Still another said, "I just got married, so I can't come."'" (Luke 14:16-20 NIV)

Sadly, these excuses stopped each of these people from going and they missed out, to their huge detriment. We must not pass over the opportunities God gives us to step out, no matter how scary or unsure the next steps may seem. When He opens a door for us, He has unlocked that door in order for us to go through it. We need to respond in obedience, not with a list of excuses.

"What He opens, no one can close; and what He closes, no one can open: 'I know all the things you do, and I have opened a door for you that no one can close. You have little strength, yet you obeyed my word and did not deny me.'" (Revelation 3:7-8 NLT)

God invites each of us to know Him, to recognise His voice and to step out on a great adventure with Him. If He has opened the door, we can trust Him to make the way for us as we step out.

"Step out, step in, step up." I had this word for a member of the Pure team several years ago. For him the step was moving from London to Liverpool, which was a big step of faith. Stepping out is not always easy. It takes surrender; it takes courage and takes obedience, but these are vital ingredients. When we step out in obedience, we give God room to do more than we ever could on our own.

22

SMALL BEGINNINGS

It was the first day of our honeymoon. We had landed exhausted but buzzing with memories of our wedding day. We were in the beautiful Caribbean and as we looked out across this paradise, all the busyness of the past few months seemed like a distant memory. We were on holiday for two weeks in a land where palm trees lined the beaches and white sand stretched into the glassy turquoise ocean. It was perfect.

We arrived at our resort in the evening, but before we'd even sat down to our first meal we had already made friends. I didn't think that making friends was really the point of a honeymoon. I had never heard of anyone talking about such a thing before. But as the days went by, we couldn't escape these two couples who seemed desperate to spend time with us. One of the couples were on honeymoon too, surely they knew better and didn't want to spend all their time with us? But evidently, they did. They wanted Nick to play tennis. They wanted me to go to the beach. They wanted to sit with us for dinner at our all-inclusive resort and, after that, they begged us to come to karaoke.

The whole thing seemed slightly ironic in the light of the address that Damian had given at our wedding service just a few days ago. He had encouraged us to protect our time together now that we were married, because he could foresee that people would want our time. We all laughed as he said this. It was a nice thing to say, but I remember wondering if it was necessarily true.

Then a few days later, this was just what was happening. With people we had never even met before!

We longed for space to just be together on the beach or by the pool by ourselves. We longed for the honeymoon where we could be indulgent and just enjoy being together.

Yet several days into our two-week break, I found myself sitting with one of these girls on the beach. As the hot sun beat down on our backs she began to pour out her story. I listened as she spoke through tears of all the things that had happened which had left her insecure and brokenhearted. The more I listened the more I longed for her to know God, to know who He had created her to be. I started to share God's truth with her, first tentatively, and then with more courage. Before I knew it, I was explaining the meaning of the cross, how she could leave all her hurt there and have a fresh start. Moments later, with tears still in her eyes, Rashida was praying with me as she made the decision to become a Christian.

I had imagined our honeymoon to be quite different, but God had a better plan. He always does. He was working where I didn't expect Him to be. Through that time away, Rashida's faith grew. We connected her to a church where she lived and later she and her husband came to visit us and came with us to our church in Liverpool. It was amazing to be a part of the journey she was on.

Even with all this happening on our honeymoon, it was hard to forget what was waiting for us when we arrived home. Nick was in his final year of university and I was still working out what Pure would look like. Another charity had suggested that we work with them to develop Pure. To me this sounded ideal, as it meant we'd be more likely to get paid right from the start, but the more we prayed and pursued this option, the less it seemed like this was what God wanted us to do.

As well as thoughts about how Pure would take shape, the other thing weighing on our minds was how we were going to afford to live this next year. God had clearly shown us that He would provide for us, but still it wasn't clear how He was going to do that.

I remember sitting by the pool reading a book and imagining what it would be like to walk on the water like Peter did, when Jesus asked him to come to Him.

"'Lord, if it's you,' Peter replied, 'tell me to come to you on the water.' 'Come,' He said. Then Peter got down out of the boat, walked on the water and came toward Jesus. But when he saw the wind, he was afraid and, beginning to sink, cried out, 'Lord, save me!' Immediately Jesus reached out His hand and caught him. 'You of little faith,' He said, 'why did you doubt?'" (Matthew 14:28-31 NIV)

I looked out at the water in the pool and wondered what would happen if I just stepped out and started to walk. Peter had done it, why couldn't I? As I thought over this passage, God showed me that He had told me to step out into what seemed impossible and I had obeyed. I had made that first phone call and it had opened up provision for the beginnings of Pure. But now I needed to keep on stepping, no matter how small those steps seemed. To continue stepping out meant I needed to keep my eyes fixed on Jesus. If the wind or storms took my focus, I would sink. I needed to have faith and not doubt what God had given me to do.

Walking on a remote beach one day, Nick and I spoke about this together. We talked about the finance we'd need to cover rent and bills for the year and calculated that we'd probably need £15,000. We wrote this figure down in the sand and drew a line under it. Then together we prayed that God would provide.

When we arrived home from honeymoon we moved into our flat. It wasn't always easy to have faith that God would provide for us, but He had shown us that He would, quite dramatically, before we were married. Now we needed to keep our eyes fixed on Him despite all the impossibility.

We lived on a shopping budget of £10 a week while Nick studied and I worked part time at a temporary job in a bank and later at a newspaper. This covered our rent only, while I spent the rest of the week working with Andrea and Kyra to set up Pure. To our amazement, God provided everything we needed to pay the bills. Money would appear through the door anonymously. Someone gave us a car, then when that broke down, another car. Little by little I was able to work more for Pure and less at the other jobs and never once did we go without. By the end of the year, we realised that in different ways God had provided the £15,000 we were in faith for. It hadn't arrived as a monthly salary, but the money had still come in.

On top of this, I had just been offered a job as a teacher in an acting school, which paid £100 per hour. This meant that I could work just a few hours each week to earn what we needed, while I gave the rest of my time to Pure.

God's provision was outrageous.

Nick and I both felt that what had happened with Rashida on our honeymoon was an encouragement for the time ahead. A challenge not to get stuck in our own ideas or expectations of what God wanted to do, but instead trust Him. Nothing was how I expected it to be. The only way we kept going that year, walking on the water of what was otherwise impossible, was by continually keeping our eyes on Jesus.

23

ACORNS TO OAKS

The sound of bass and underground beats filled the studio as Matt laid down the drums for the track. We were excited to be recording our first song and it was slowly coming together with a blend of Kyra rapping and me singing out the lyrics:

"Don't you know that He loves you, don't you know that He made you, don't you know that He's the only one that will ever understand? What you gonna do He loves you, what you gonna do, He made you. It's up to you." (Osgood, Evans, Hodge, McIntyre)

It was a classic.

The one thing the three of us had in common when we started Pure was that we'd all had some experience of writing songs and performing in school assemblies. It seemed like starting a band was an obvious starting place for us.

We stayed with my parents while we recorded the song at a friend's studio in York. One morning I awoke to discover a pile of cat vomit on the floor. Eager to be a good hostess, I didn't want Andrea or Kyra to see the vomit, so I tried to clean it up as quickly and quietly as I could. But I couldn't stomach the smell or look of the vomit and to my embarrassment just as Andrea came downstairs I vomited on top of the cat vomit!

Andrea was a vet nurse by trade and quickly cleaned up both mine and the cat's vomit. It was a bonding experience before we recorded the first demo version of "Don't You Know?"

We took this song back to Liverpool and rehearsed it with our backing dancers, but we never ended up performing it. "Don't You Know?" was used in many schools in York by a band called Overtone, but God had other plans for Pure.

Kyra moved away from Liverpool after a year and Andrea and I continued to write and record more songs, which we performed in school assemblies across Liverpool. We were well received by the schools we went into, but deep down I knew this wasn't everything Pure was meant to be. How could we see lasting change in these young people's lives if we were there for just one assembly and then left? Surely there was more we could do.

Around this time we were invited to start a girl's group, which would deal with issues of identity in a local high school. It was here that we began to really do what Pure had set out to do. We worked closely with Jo Wells, a youth worker from a local church, to develop a term-long programme which helped students to unpack who they were and how they saw themselves. Identity was right at the core of what we felt God had asked us to address with girls and this group was amazing. Once the course finished we made plans to run similar courses in other schools and this is how Pure's Impact groups were born.

I think somewhere along the way we had felt it was important that we were doing something "big" that was known, seen and recognised. But, actually, it's from little acorns that mighty oak trees grow. We needed to be content with small beginnings, keeping the bigger picture in mind, while we obediently worked at what God had given us to do.

One day, just before we were about to go and lead an impact group, Andrea and I were sitting in a park praying together. As we looked up at the numerous oak trees around us we felt God say that the seeds we were sowing today through these Impact groups would grow into oak trees. Right now we saw acorns, but one day they would become oaks. We began to laugh and joke about the years to come when we would be old ladies and we would look back on the oaks that had grown out of seemingly small and unglamorous work. This perspective was so encouraging.

Whenever you start something new it can be easy to feel that things aren't making progress quickly enough. But there is something wonderful about small beginnings.

Andrea and I had big ideas about the lives that Pure could impact and the things that we could do, and sometimes it felt like things weren't moving quickly enough. At that time God was asking us to do all we could with the opportunities that we had been given, trusting that as we were faithful, He would give us more.

"Do not despise these small beginnings, for the Lord rejoices to see the work begin." (Zechariah 4:10 NLT)

No one likes small beginnings, especially when it seems like things remain small for a long time. But every big thing starts small and it takes patience to make it grow. Lots of people give up prematurely on a dream God has given them, because they feel what they are doing is not working, when in truth they've only just begun.

Almost everyone who has gone on to do great things started small. Take billionaire entrepreneur Richard Branson, for example. Branson's first business venture was a magazine called *Student*, which he started when he was 17. Not many people know about this magazine. It wasn't big or well known and a few years later he tried something else. In 1970, he set up a mail order record business and by 1972 he opened a chain of record stores known as Virgin Records, later known as Virgin Megastores. By the 1980s the Virgin brand grew to include Virgin Atlantic and now the Virgin group comprises more than 400 companies.

We all have to start small and it takes time to find a niche. We need to be prepared to keep going and pursue the plan that we have, but simultaneously be open and flexible to change how we are outworking that plan.

"Sometimes when I consider what tremendous consequences come from little things, I am tempted to think there are no little things." – Bruce Barton

At the start of something new it's tempting to look around at what other people are doing and become distracted and disheartened at the task in front of us, until eventually we just give up. There is no shortage of people to compare ourselves with. It's hard not to get demoralised when we're constantly bombarded with pictures and messages about how amazing other people's lives are through social media. The challenge for us is to focus our attention on Jesus as He calls out to us and to be obedient to what God has given us to do.

The verse in Zechariah tells us not to despise these early days. If we have the right perspective we'll see what God sees and God rejoices in our small beginnings. Our small beginnings mean a step of faith has been taken and a willingness to obey God demonstrated. We aren't able to ride on past successes, because we have none. We are not confident in ourselves, we have not yet achieved anything. This small and weak place is the best place for us to be – and it's here that God can use us.

I would say that Pure still is a small beginning – there is so much I believe God wants to do and grow through Pure. Even now, I have to be content in the small beginning of where we are today. We have grown from the days when we started those impact groups, we have shrunk back, and we have grown again. At times it has seemed like we've taken two steps forward and one back, but I've come to realise that God "prunes" us in order to keep us healthy as we go along. A recently pruned fruit tree can look like it has been decimated beyond repair, and yet if it is not pruned, it will eventually wither and die. Pruning is never easy, but it is biblical and vital for our growth.

"I am the true vine, and My Father is the vinedresser. Every branch in Me that does not bear fruit, He takes away; and every branch that bears fruit, He prunes it so that it may bear more fruit." (John 15:1-2 NAS)

In the pruning seasons I always remind myself that it is so we will be more fruitful. His plan is for us to bear *even more* fruit. As an organisation, each time Pure has been pruned, we have grown back bigger as a result.

Through each season the most important element is knowing that God is in charge and that He grows small beginnings bigger according to His timing. Each time I am tempted to feel discouraged, I love to remember that from little acorns, mighty oak trees grow.

24

DELUGE

The glass in the hallway rattled as the front door slammed shut. Joy had only been living with us for a few days now and we were concerned. Driving down the road a little later that day, we saw her walking on her own under the bridge near our house. She had her hat pulled down so far that it almost covered her eyes. She looked like a completely different person to the girl we had known.

Just a few months ago she had been in Australia at the same time as us. Amid the fun we had together I knew something was wrong and it was getting progressively worse. A few weeks after our trip, I noticed that her wrists were bound with bracelets and pieces of material that weren't usually there. Aware that she had been struggling with self-harming for years, I asked her why she was wearing all these bracelets. Eventually she told me that she had tried to end her life a few days ago and the bracelets were covering up the wounds.

Nick and I discussed what we could do to help and decided to invite her to live with us for a while. However, we knew that if she agreed to live with us, it would have to be on our terms. No cutting, no suicide attempts. If she did that she would have to go. We hoped that a new environment would help her deal with her emotions more positively and that we'd be able to give her some extra support if she needed it.

But it didn't go very smoothly. Just a few days after she moved in with us, a break-up meant that things took a turn for the worse. Instead of opening up about the pain she felt, Joy shut down completely. It was like an impenetrable dark cloak surrounded her and nothing we could say or do seemed to break through it. It seemed all I could do was watch as the pain pushed her to her very limit.

Alongside the work I was doing with Pure, God was challenging me through bringing people into my life from every direction who were all struggling with the very same life-controlling issues that He was calling Pure to address. It felt a little like the clouds had opened to release a deluge of broken lives all around me. Many times I felt completely unequipped to help.

I had so much to learn and God was teaching me on the job. For some, like Joy, the issue was self-harm. For others it was an eating disorder that they were finding it impossible to overcome.

The night that we saw Joy walking on her own with her hat pulled down over her eyes was the night where I thought she might try to take her life again. When she returned home, I went to her room to check if she was okay and she seemed like she was hiding something.

Later I heard a rattling coming from the bathroom that sounded like packets of pills being opened up. Was she in there taking an overdose? Someone else I had mentored had tried to take an overdose in our house before. My heart began to pound again as I ran up the stairs. Thankfully I was wrong this time.

I loved this girl and the others I had helped in the past. I desperately wanted to make sure I was doing the right thing for them and not saying anything that could damage them or make things worse. The leaders in my church helped me look at the best way we could support these women. Sometimes I encouraged them to seek counselling or go to their doctors for help; other times we just sat together over countless cups of coffee and tea, trying to make sense of who God was in the situations that they faced.

There was no easy fix or clear-cut solution. No prayer formula that could zap the problems away. The prescription was time, time and more time. All I knew to do was trust that God would work through our conversations and love each one through the ups and downs, regardless of what progress they made.

It was good to remember I was not alone. More importantly, I needed to remember that God was the one who loved each of these girls more than I ever could. He knew them. He knew what they faced and what was happening within them. He was their Father and He was able to impact each situation.

And the situations just became more and more challenging. People who I came into contact with were dealing with all kinds of issues. Some self-harmed, some took drugs, others regularly had sex with strangers and found themselves in dangerous situations. These situations required Nick and I to make decisions we'd never thought we'd have to make...

The phone trilled in the darkness. It was the early hours. Nick and I had been fast asleep when we were jolted awake by the sound. Nick answered groggily, before handing the phone to me. Half asleep, I answered:

"Hello...?"

"Help me!" a rasping voice whispered. "I'm in trouble. Can you come? Can you rescue me?"

How could we respond to a call like that? Surely we had no other choice but to go and save them? A few days after this call, we discussed the situation with our church leaders and I was surprised to hear that they didn't think that we should be responding to every midnight phone call.

"But what if we hadn't answered the phone?" I questioned. "What if they'd been harmed because we hadn't gone to get them?"

It wasn't our responsibility to protect each person,   they said. We'd burn out if we kept on going like this. It was time to put some boundaries in place for our own protection.

This conversation stuck with me over the week. As I mulled it over in my mind, a thought occurred to me that I hadn't considered before: "Who is their protector? Me or God?"

As I stopped to think about this, I realised that God was well able to protect each person without my assistance. I was not created to be superwoman and I was not the only person God could work through. At times this meant calling the police and always ensuring that good safeguarding practice was in place in all we did.

This was a lesson I needed to learn as more and more girls crossed my path. As I sat with them they began to pour out their heartbreaking stories. The struggles they were facing were nothing like the ones I'd faced. Nothing I could say or do would "fix" them. Very often I felt completely ill-equipped to help, so I began to train in Counselling and Transactional Analysis to strengthen what I could bring.

After an event I was speaking at, a girl began to tell me of a horrific incident that had happened only the night before. She had agreed to babysit for someone when a male friend of hers asked if he could join her. On their own in someone else's house with the child asleep, there was no way to stop him when his advances took an unwanted direction. He raped her that night and she blamed herself for what had happened. She was so ashamed that she hadn't said a word to anyone yet, until now when she poured her story out to me.

Another girl, during a very difficult time, had drunk too much one night. A guy she was with had offered to take her home, but when they arrived, he took advantage of her; her virginity lost, without consent. Confusion had clouded her mind. Was it her fault? She went over the details of that night countless times, tripping up over the weeds of shame that were wrapping themselves around her heart until she finally came to the realisation she had been raped.

The stories were countless. So many lives wrapped up in pain, longing desperately to be set free.

As I gave all my concern and anxiety about not knowing how to handle each situation to God, I realised that it was not my job to heal these women. God did not need me to protect them or even to do some "great" thing. He just needed me to love them, listen to Him, learn and be obedient as He led.

25

REACHING FOR THE IMPOSSIBLE

"I need to tell you something."

Sophie eyes shifted around the room. She was looking at her nails, the cup, her journal, anywhere but at me. On the couch beside her I waited as she gathered her thoughts. I could tell she was struggling to form the words. When the silence became too awkward for either of us to handle, we started chatting about something else, until eventually she was ready to tell me about the relationship she had just come out of with another girl. It had been intense, dependent and toxic.

As we chatted further it was clear that Sophie was struggling with her sexuality. It wasn't a black and white issue for her. She didn't only like girls, she frequently dated guys too. She had lost her virginity before she felt ready to and the truth was that she was uncertain what her feelings were for either sex. What she needed now was space to explore who she was. She needed a place where she felt accepted just as she was, space where she could be open about her thoughts and feelings which had been bottled up for so long. So we provided that. No judgment, just love and time to talk and pray.

More and more challenging situations arose. Girls who feared relationships, who had suffered abuse. Girls who were haunted by self-loathing and found hatred every place they looked. Girls whose minds were drowning in dark thoughts.

There were girls who believed they were unlovable and were desperately trying to find the love they craved. Others who couldn't bring themselves to trust that God had a good plan for them and moved from relationship to relationship to ensure they were not left alone to contemplate the hollowness they felt deep within.

The more I talked to them, loved them, spent time with them, the more I learnt how little I knew and yet how mighty God is. I knew that I did not have a chance of trying to solve any of these problems and any time I began to think that I could help or sort any one of these women out, I was in grave danger.

It was not about me. I didn't need to be perfect. I just needed to obey and put in place safe practice. So that's what I did. I ran a small group each week where there was space to worship, pray and study the Bible, and I also tried to meet up with each girl regularly, to talk and pray together.

Slowly, I realised that the one thing I could give these girls was my faith to reach for the impossible in their situations. I didn't have all the answers or know very much. But I did have faith in a God who I knew could move mountains. As I stood with them and believed for what seemed impossible, as I told them stories about what God had previously done, I saw Him do amazing things in their lives.

This was a time of learning on the job, seeking advice from others who were more experienced than me and I learnt a lot. I brought every new situation I faced to God and He would guide me through.

As I spent time reading the Bible, I realised that so much of what I needed to learn could be found by studying the gospels and learning from Jesus.

"So Jesus explained, 'I tell you the truth, the Son can do nothing by himself. He does only what he sees the Father doing. Whatever the Father does, the Son also does. For the Father loves the Son and shows him everything he is doing. In fact, the Father will show him how to do even greater works than healing

this man. Then you will truly be astonished.'" (John 5:19-20 NLT)

Jesus did nothing by Himself. He only did what He saw the Father do. The most important thing for me to discover was what God was doing and find a way to join in with that.

"And a woman was there who had been subject to bleeding for twelve years, but no one could heal her. She came up behind him and touched the edge of his cloak, and immediately her bleeding stopped. 'Who touched me?' Jesus asked. When they all denied it, Peter said, 'Master, the people are crowding and pressing against you.' But Jesus said, 'Someone touched me; I know that power has gone out from me.' Then the woman, seeing that she could not go unnoticed, came trembling and fell at his feet. In the presence of all the people, she told why she had touched him and how she had been instantly healed. Then he said to her, 'Daughter, your faith has healed you. Go in peace.'" (Luke 8:43-48 NIV)

Another thing God taught me during this time was that He wanted these women to reach for Him themselves. It was my job to encourage them and build their faith to approach God. With the woman who was bleeding, it was not until Jesus felt power go out from Him into her and He asked the question, that He recognised she was being healed. Her faith to reach out and touch Him was enough. Encouraging this kind of faith to rise up in others was the most important thing I could do.

Through it all God kept reminding me that it wasn't about what I could do. I wasn't the only one He could use.

* * *

I arrived at our church, ready to speak at the evening service. I was a little nervous about leaving the house that night because it was only four months after our daughter Lois was born and I'd left Nick to put her and our son Joshua to bed on his own for the first time. But I had prepared my talk and was excited about what God had given me to say.

I was just about to get up to speak when I handed my phone to the person leading the meeting, asking them to let me know if Nick called. As I did, I noticed a message from Nick flash up on the screen:

"Come home immediately, Lois won't stop crying. I don't know what is wrong. We need you."

Showing the meeting leader the message, I ran to the back of the church while he improvised an extended time of prayer. I tried to call Nick repeatedly, but got no answer. I had a choice to make and I needed to decide quickly. Would I stay and preach or would I go home? I apologised and left the church, my family had to come first.

When I got home I found that everyone was fine. I had misunderstood Nick's text. He had meant for me to leave immediately after the talk. Although glad that all was okay, I was also disappointed. I'd been excited about the message I'd prepared to bring that night. I had felt God's presence on me in the worship, then I'd had to leave the service and just walk away.

But there was a lesson to be learnt. All the time and prayer I had put into preparing the talk was not wasted, God still did what He had planned that evening and Nic Harding, our pastor, stepped in and gave a great talk.

I realised afresh that evening that God does not depend on me. He is well able to work in situations when I'm not there!

When Jesus was told that his friend Lazarus was sick, all his friends expected him to rush to his side. But instead, He didn't start the journey until two days later. By the time He'd arrived Lazarus had been dead for four days. To His friends it seemed like Jesus didn't care enough to hurry over to see him in time, but the truth was He had a far better plan in mind and Lazarus was raised from the dead (John 11:3-43).

This story showed me again that it is not about us doing things in the right time. Other people's healing does not hinge on our timing, but on God's – who isn't constricted by our timescales. This freed me up to understand that even if I'm not available to help someone, God is big enough to work beyond and outside of that. He is able to resurrect the dead and nothing is beyond Him. It is all on Him and not on me.

One of the most important things I've learnt is that Jesus knew how to prioritise and set boundaries. He knew when to go up a mountain and get refreshed in God's presence. He knew when to stay and when to go. Most importantly, He knew He needed time with His Father.

"But the news about Him was spreading even farther, and large crowds were gathering to hear Him and to be healed of their sicknesses. But Jesus Himself would often slip away to the wilderness and pray." (Luke 5:15-16 NAS)

In the midst of busyness and high demand, the temptation is to work harder. To "slip away" can feel almost a little self-indulgent. But this is the most important thing we can do.

There was so much for me to learn in these three areas and it's something I'm still challenged by today. Through all of this, I learnt that God would never forsake these people or me. As I sought Him, loved them and believed that with God nothing was impossible, faith pushed through and we saw the miraculous happen. Sometimes these stories didn't end as I hoped they would, but more times than not, I saw God bring incredible freedom into people's lives.

26

ENDURANCE

It was an ordinary October morning at the bank where I worked opening new accounts for students. There was the usual banter among the staff and a small queue of students forming by the desk when suddenly there was a loud crash and smoke filled the air. The bank became a flurry of panic. Amidst the screams of staff members I was pulled into a back room before the safety doors were locked. We sat huddled in the back of that bank for what seemed like hours. Eventually, we were informed that the bank next door had been ram raided. The police didn't know where the armed robbers were and there was a risk that they were in our building. At the same time they were concerned that the car used in the ram raid might blow up. We were stuck in the bank and I was terrified.

Nick, who was at the university nearby, saw smoke rising from the bank from his lecture window and received a text from me saying: "Bank been ram raided, stuck in back, car might blow, please pray." He ran all the way down to find me, but the whole area was cordoned off with police tape and surrounded by police in white forensic suits who would not let him past.

I was working at this bank to support Nick and I while he studied and I set up Pure. It was the first in a line of jobs which would provide some income to cover our rent and bills. Eventually, we were let out of the bank and thankfully no one was hurt, but the whole experience really shook me. I realised the dangers of where I worked and I didn't want to go back. I began to question what I was doing and whether God really did want me to work there.

I'd enjoyed seeing the students and doing all I could to be a listening ear for them. Much to the frustration of my managers, I gave myself the express purpose of encouraging them not to take out a credit card, so they wouldn't get into debt. But deep down I knew there was more for me.

Now I realise that through this job, and the ones that would come afterwards, God was developing my character. It was a time through which I needed to persevere and learn as much as I could along the way. There is something about learning to work hard and keep going at a job you find difficult that builds work ethic. Jobs like this are not to be despised. They are opportunities to grow and to prepare for what God has in store for us next.

The next job offer I had was for a temporary role as a copy editor at the *Echo*, Liverpool's local newspaper. I liked the idea of working at a newspaper and having a title like "editor", so with some excitement I made my way to my first day on the job there dressed in my finest work clothes and heels.

On arrival I was met by a guy, slightly older than me, who was to show me the ropes before he left. The first thing he said to me was: "You're not a lad."

I was flummoxed by this statement. I was pretty sure it was obvious I was female and I had no idea why he was saying this. He looked me up and down and then said, "Why did they send you? You haven't got much muscle."

I looked at his arms, a little self conscious that he was making such an observation, but mostly confused about what that had to do with the job. It didn't become clear until I followed him down to the printing room where all the newspapers were stored and he began to show me what I was there to do. My job was to collect newspapers and move them upstairs to an office. It was a lifting job. The muscles suddenly made sense.

I loathed this job from the first day. I've always hated the feel of newspaper on my hands and now I spent all day carrying and leafing through them to find articles for customers who wanted copies. Every other person in my office was male and much older than me. I felt really out of place, but I persevered and got on with the job. As I did, I looked for ways I could go the extra mile or give glory to God in the details.

I often struggled with the lack of focus and purpose in the jobs I did during the first few years of Pure. But through each job, each humbling experience, God was teaching me to keep going and trust in Him, even when I didn't understand it all.

Around this time I saw an advertisement for a full time job as a Performing Arts Lecturer. I knew that God wanted me to be focusing on Pure, but I was so tempted by the idea of a job title that actually related to what I was trained to do and a decent salary, that I applied anyway. I was offered an interview, then on the morning I was due to go I realised that I was being disobedient. A job title and a salary had become more important to me than obeying God and I needed to let that go. In the end I decided not to go to the interview.

All through this time the work with Pure continued slowly. Initially, we met in the evenings or worked half days around other jobs. After a few months of working at the *Echo*, I was offered a part-time job as a receptionist, which meant I spent two days a week working with Andrea as we started Impact groups and led school assemblies

A year later, in 2005, two more people joined our team. It was so encouraging to me that these two amazing women believed in Pure enough to commit to giving their time to it. Around the same time we moved into new offices in a house called Strawberry Fields, where a couple were starting a 24/7 prayer room. So much of what we had done had started in prayer, it was exciting to see God position our offices in a house designated to around-the-clock prayer.

But around each victory there were new challenges to face. As the team grew and we moved into our new offices, Nick and I were taken to court.

We had just bought our first house and I was excited to hand the keys of our small flat back to our landlord. We had meticulously cleaned the flat and even though it was my birthday I wanted to hand the keys back to the landlord personally, as I thought he would be pleased to see how well we'd looked after it.

Instead of the gratitude I expected, he began to complain about how bad the flat looked. I was taken aback by his reaction. I knew what he was saying wasn't true. He'd always seemed like a nice man, I didn't understand why he was suddenly lying.

A few days later, he sent us a bill for over £1,000 listing all the damages to the flat that we had so carefully looked after. We were shocked. This was a huge amount of money to us at the time. No correspondence from us seemed to help or change his mind, so eventually we were taken to court. My Dad had acted as our guarantor so he was dragged along too.

There was no way we could pay the bill, nor did we feel we should. As we'd prayed in the run up to the court case we felt God speak to us through this verse:

"He will make your innocence as clear as the dawn, and the justice of your cause will shine like the noonday sun." (Psalm 37:6 NLT)

We were nervous on the day of the hearing. When our landlord arrived he looked intimidatingly organised with his huge colour coded file. But as we brought our case to the judge, every point our landlord made seemed confused and petty. At one point he started to say how unacceptable it was that we had not used foil on the grill pan. Here the judge stepped in. Looking over her glasses imperiously she said, "I don't use foil on my grill pan, Mr Andrews. Do you think I am unacceptable?"

It was a glorious moment and we left the courthouse with the £1,000 bill cancelled. Instead, our landlord was ordered to pay us. God had made our innocence shine like the noonday sun and we were so relieved.

Then a few days later someone slashed all the tyres on our car, which meant all the money that had been paid back to us was spent on replacing them.

I believe that times like these were distractions from all the good things God was doing. It took endurance and courage to keep going even when it seemed like everything was stacked up against us. Still, all of this time was key in building resilience in me as I continued to pioneer the work of Pure.

I learnt that not everyone would like me or praise what I was doing. Some people would set out to be unkind, to attack and to criticise. In these times I had to fix my eyes on what God said about me and keep going.

By March of that year Pure was incorporated as a company and charity in its own right. We could apply for funding and charge for charitable services that we delivered. We developed our first production which addressed body image and eating disorders and began to perform it in schools. From here our Theatre in Education work was born. It was an exciting season of early mornings, McDonald's breakfasts and rehearsals as we went into schools to perform and lead workshops, and we began to develop our second production, *Hold Me*.

A few months later, Andrea, the other founding member of Pure, decided it was time to move on. I knew it was the right thing for her because the day before she told me, I felt God say that she was going to leave whilst I was doing the washing up. But it didn't mean I wasn't devastated. When Andrea left Pure, it almost felt like she was breaking up with me. I wondered if she didn't believe in the vision any more, which caused me to doubt myself.

Yet, God used this time so powerfully to build endurance for the future. I learnt that the vision for Pure was built on nothing apart from God. He was the one who would make it grow and bring the right people. I needed to continue to trust Him.

Section 4
THE CHALLENGES OF FLYING

The bird climbs up, up, up, growing in strength with each journey into the sky. High up in the air it soars on wind currents and learns to fly in formation with others.

27

COLLISIONS

Learning to fly comes with all kinds of crashes and collisions along the way. Sometimes these collisions are God-ordained moments of connection. Lives collide in one instant and the effect of these moments ripple on into the future. Other collisions can be the result of opposition, designed to distract us from the task God has given us to do. And sometimes, these crashes are the result of trying something new and getting it wrong...

Listening to the sound of the clock ticking was driving me to distraction. I had so much to do before I needed to collect my son, Joshua, from school and each tick told me that another second had disappeared. Tick, tick, tick... Then my phone began to ring. Groaning, I looked to see who was calling me, hoping that I could ignore it, but it was one of Pure's key benefactors, I had to answer.

In the run up to a big event, I had convinced this very kind benefactor to provide branded merchandise for the team. To save time for everyone else, I had decided to handle the whole thing myself and in doing so had made a serious error. Assuming that the project was being overseen by one of his staff, I didn't really spend much time looking into the detail until I found out that the merchandise had cost more than double what our benefactor had said he would give. My lack of attention to detail and failure to delegate in this instance had meant a serious breach in our relationship.

Now he was on the other end of the phone telling me that one of his staff was very upset that the bill for the merchandise was way over what had been agreed. The call ended and I was left in floods of tears. I feared I'd ruined the relationship and, more than that, I worried that the benefactor would think I was being greedy, when in reality I had thought the price had been authorised. It was my mistake. My mistake because I had failed to pay attention to the detail or to delegate this task to someone else.

I was so angry with myself that I had made this mistake. But mistakes happen and when they happen it is how we deal with them that matters. In this case, I did everything I could to correct my oversight. I took responsibility and paid the excess on the merchandise, apologised profusely, and looked for ways to show how sorry I was. In the end we came out of this with a stronger relationship and further developments that have been such a blessing to Pure.

I can be a bit of a perfectionist. I want to get things right every time. To have the right attitude, make the right decisions, and treat people in the right way. But I am an imperfect human being, steeped in weakness, who God chooses in His grace to use. He doesn't use me because He thinks I am perfect. He well knows how flawed I am. He chooses to use me because I am weak. Mistakes are an opportunity to learn, to grow with humility, and they can actually help us grow into the person God has created us to be. The sooner I realise it is not about me being right and embrace my mistakes the better.

Part of the beauty of flying is that we don't do it alone. God calls others into the adventure with us so that when we fall they are there to help us shake off the dust and learn from our mistakes. It's easy to become so focused on what we're doing that we fail to recognise the people God has brought into our lives to work with.

To fly in formation with others we need to see the bigger

picture. As we collide with the lives of others, we need to keep asking God what He is doing. Why has He brought us into connection with each person and how do we take our place in formation with the others around us?

Becky Murphy was one of the first members of our team. We were in a meeting one day when I asked her where she saw herself in five year's time. She knew immediately and began to describe a dance school that she had dreamt of running as a little girl. At the time I was teaching acting at a stage school and was frustrated at how much pressure was placed on each pupil by their parents and the Director of the school. This pressure to lose weight, to look a certain way and to succeed, seemed to come without any thought to their encouragement and development as an individual.

As Becky talked about her dream, I wondered whether God might have a plan in all of this. Later, I spoke to a friend of mine who taught singing at this same stage school. He and I talked and prayed about it and then talked with Becky about the possibility of setting up a different kind of performance school. We prayed some more and through this our Creative Arts School was born. The idea behind the school is to see children and young people grow in confidence and self-esteem as they are taught skills in drama, singing and dance. It had a small beginning with just six pupils in the first session, but Becky did an incredible job of growing it quickly to 40 pupils.

Starting a Creative Arts School was not at the forefront of my mind at this time, it was only when Becky mentioned it that I saw how the dream for Pure and her dream to run a dance school could collide. Now, the school is one of our longest running projects and we've seen some great results. Pupils who have attended our weekly classes have grown in confidence at school, in relationship with peers, and in their own academic achievements. One CAS parent told us,

"The difference in my child's confidence on the whole has been fantastic to watch – school is a happier place, parties are a little less overwhelming and she sings out loud to me with a gorgeous little voice."

This wasn't the only time that other people's dreams collided within Pure to form a much bigger picture. As Pure grew, more and more people joined our team with new vision and ideas brewing in their hearts. At one stage we were praying to see Pure grow nationally and four people we had never met before got in touch with us asking if they could join the team and start something in their city. God was working beyond what we could see so that our lives could collide with theirs. It's always so exciting when God brings people together in most unexpected ways, to do something they would never have considered on their own.

As we learn to fly, we'll all have crashes, but what is important is how we deal with them. Is there something to learn? Is there an opportunity to work with someone new? Or is it another kind of crash, a distraction and reminder of the opposition we face when taking new ground?

28

CRASHES

The smell of burning rubber on tarmac. A car door bent out of shape. From a crackling police radio a voice churned out a series of numbers and instructions. Just a few seconds, one mistake and CRASH. Two lives collide in the balance of life and death...

I was driving back to our office in South Liverpool from a meeting in the city centre. Music blared through the stereo as I thought about what exciting developments could come out of the meeting I had just left and the new team member I was on my way to interview. The team was growing and new opportunities were opening everywhere.

Elsewhere, another driver had just dropped his girlfriend off at a clinic. The inevitability of what was to come had grown a numb silence between them. This day had been preceded by a tennis ball debate. Backwards and forwards: should they keep the baby or not? Part of him wanted to say yes, but the fear of what would this mean for his life and hers spoke louder. He had offered to stay with her at the clinic, but was a little relieved when she told him to go. He hated the idea of what was about to happen.

Now, in between two lanes of traffic waiting to turn, tears blurred his vision. Emotion overtook him as he thought about the past few weeks and the reality of what was happening to his girlfriend right now. Each lane of traffic racing past reminded him of the tennis ball debates they'd had. They had made their decision logically, hadn't they? Every reason that had flown back and forth crowded into his mind and smudged the traffic into a blur. Without looking, he put his foot down on the pedal to try and escape them. CRASH!

He hit me side on. My mind went into a blank haze as my car lurched with a sickening thud into the pavement. Eventually it stopped moving. Shaking from the impact I slowly pushed the door open and stumbled out. Adrenaline took over as I saw the car that had hit me start to drive away. I ran down the street after him. "STOP! What were you doing? You didn't look!" I shouted. He pulled over and stepped out of his car.

He nodded, eyes swimming with tears. I was expecting a fight. Instead here I was listening to a stranger trying to find the words to tell me that his girlfriend was about to have an abortion.

My heart went out to him. No longer caught up in my own fury, I swapped insurance details with him and we went our separate ways. Shaken by the impact, tears streamed down my face as later, after speaking to the police, I drove my car back to the office. I wasn't just crying from the shock of the crash, but for that man, his girlfriend and their baby who was probably being aborted right now.

On the day of that crash I was on my way to audition a new team member, Abi. When I arrived back at the office, shaken and in tears, our chair of trustees suggested that we cancel, but I couldn't let that happen. Something in me sensed that this interview was a crucial moment and although circumstances were trying to stop it from happening, I needed to push through. Abi joined us as a performer initially and quickly became an integral part of our team. But the day of that collision always stuck with me and the issue of abortion struck a chord in my heart.

To this day we spend a lot of time in schools talking about relationships and in almost every session, questions about sex and contraception crop up. In earlier sessions, sometimes we would ask pupils what they would do if they fell pregnant now. Unfazed, many responded that they would have an abortion. Pressing them a little further, we asked if they knew how abortions worked. When they replied with a lot less certainty, we began to discover that this was an area where there was a desperate need of education. On the day of that collision I was reminded of how much of a taboo subject abortion really is. It was an issue that affected so many people and it needed to be brought out into the open.

God had used our past performances in amazing ways to help people share hidden pain for the first time. At a Christian conference called Spring Harvest we had seen a venue crowded out with people desperate to talk about their own struggles with eating disorders after watching our performance of *Mirror Mirror*. We knew that using theatre in this way was a tool that God was really using to enable people to talk about hidden issues.

An idea started forming for a way we could address this. Working closely with a Doctor and a counsellor to ensure what we made was both educational and helpful for people who may already have had an abortion, we began to develop a new performance which allowed us to address this taboo subject. Abi ended up taking one of the lead roles.

As I look back, I can see that out of that crash God caused good to come and I have seen Him do this time and time again in different ways.

"You intended to harm me, but God intended it for good to accomplish what is now being done, the saving of many lives." (Genesis 50:20 NIV)

Earlier in Genesis we read about the journey that precedes this statement. Joseph experienced crashes and collisions, with his brothers selling him into slavery, his boss's wife accusing him of rape and then he was forgotten and left in prison. Even when Joseph was later promoted to an influential position, his response to all the crashes, all the hurt and harm, was to see that God intended good through it.

There is a challenge in every crash and collision to look for how God intends good to come about from it.

Months later, we were doing a week-long booking in a school on the Wirral, a borough on the outskirts of Liverpool. Momentum had been building throughout the week and the team was working really well together. We had a lot of fun and there was a real sense of God working in each session.

On one occasion, Andy was jumping around and dancing while worshipping, when a teacher walked in. The rest of us stopped, but because he had his back to the door, he just continued. It was very funny.

On the last day of the booking someone crashed into my car as we were about to park. It was the car of another Christian schools worker, who was coming into the school that day, and we managed to settle it pretty quickly, but still it wasn't a great start to the day. However, that day went on to be amazing. After our final performance of the week, the school chaplain gave me the opportunity to explain the gospel to the entire school. When I finished, and the pupils were dismissed, a number of them came up to ask us how they could become Christians.

The next day, the school hall was being used for a Christian youth event. As the leaders came to set up for the night ahead, they found gold dust on the seats.

Around that time there were a number of occasions when similar things happened. Sometimes feathers would fall in times of worship. Sometimes a gold dust substance would appear on people's hands or even in a cloud and we began to realise it was

God's presence showing up in tangible ways. There was such a sense of the presence of God being poured out through that week in the school. It was an incredible confirmation of all He was doing.

Throughout the Bible God's presence shows up in all kinds of different ways. He appears in a burning bush when He speaks to Moses, as a pillar of cloud by day and fire by night for the Israelites. In the New Testament when Stephen encounters God it says his face shone bright like an angel.

God is uncontainable and not limited by our understanding or expectations. Sometimes He'll show up in bizarre ways. When this happens the important thing is to keep our eyes fixed on Jesus, to worship only Him and not the experience.

Setbacks can potentially prevent us taking the ground God has for us, putting us off, discouraging us and lessening our faith. Over the years I've always felt that if things become hard going, God must have something so good planned that the enemy is putting up a bit of resistance. In these times it's really important to pray and worship the Lord, because our praise itself is powerful. It breaks resistance.

"Around midnight Paul and Silas were praying and singing hymns to God, and the other prisoners were listening. Suddenly, there was a massive earthquake, and the prison was shaken to its foundations. All the doors immediately flew open, and the chains of every prisoner fell off!" (Acts 16:25-26 NLT)

I love the response that Paul and Silas have while imprisoned. Resistance has come against them as they are sharing the gospel and they have been put in jail. How do they respond? They praise – and look what happens! Praise breaks our prison of resistance.

Recently on a journey to speak at a Christian conference at the other end of the country, the weather was so bad that a huge pot hole formed on a major motorway, closing down three of the four lanes. What should have been a five-hour journey turned into ten hours. As we spent three hours at a complete stand still, I honestly wondered if we would get to the conference on time. But instead of getting angry or frustrated we decided to worship instead. As we were sitting there, we began to pray and sing, welcoming the presence of the Lord beyond the resistance, the impossibility, the gridlock that was all around us. Thankfully, we made the conference just in time.

With every step forward there is a struggle to take new ground. But as we continue to pray and seek God, He always makes a way. When the crash times come, this is not a time to give up, it is a time to grow, a time to learn; a time to pray, worship and, as Nehemiah said, to let the joy of the Lord be our strength (Nehemiah 8:10).

In the book of Nehemiah in the Old Testament we read about a time when the walls of the once glorious city of Jerusalem have fallen to ruin and how Nehemiah sets about rebuilding them. There is a passage in this book through which God has often spoken to me regarding Pure. In the first chapter of Nehemiah we see Nehemiah's heart breaking for the walls of his city. The walls of the city are often seen as a symbol for the core principles that the city lives by. Whenever I read Nehemiah I feel a similar stir in my heart and a call for Pure to rebuild the walls in our nations; to see God's principles and values restored in our society; to see marriage become sacred again and for young men and women to save sex for marriage.

As Nehemiah cries out to God he is instructed to start the mammoth task of rebuilding the walls. It's a risky job that could cost him his life, but he is obedient to the call, draws a team of people around him and he begins rebuilding the walls. But the journey is not straightforward for him. In fact, he meets a lot of attack and opposition along the way:

"Then I said to them, 'You see the trouble we are in: Jerusalem lies in ruins, and its gates have been burned with fire. Come, let us rebuild the wall of Jerusalem, and we will no longer be in disgrace.' I also told them about the gracious hand of my God on me and what the king had said to me. They replied, 'Let us start rebuilding.' So they began this good work. But when Sanballat the Horonite, Tobiah the Ammonite official and Geshem the Arab heard about it, they mocked and ridiculed us. 'What is this you are doing?' they asked. 'Are you rebelling against the king?' I answered them by saying, 'The God of heaven will give us success. We his servants will start rebuilding.'" (Nehemiah 2:17-20 NIV)

I love the way that Nehemiah is so focused on the job in hand. He doesn't doubt himself. He isn't buffeted by others' ridicule and mocking. Instead he declares in faith that the Lord will give him success. He is confident that his work is the Lord's and that God will give him success.

When opposition comes we need to remember, like Nehemiah, that God is the one who will give us success. He is with us and will make the way ahead clear. He can turn around each setback for good as we keep our eyes fixed on Him.

29

BURN OUT

I woke up with a start. Velvety darkness met my eyes as they flew open. My heart was galloping. Loud, thick thuds at the pace of racing horses, as though I had just completed a 100 metre sprint. Panicking, I woke Nick. He could feel my racing heart as soon as he touched me. We didn't know what to do. Call an ambulance? Go to the hospital? We weren't sure, so we lay there in the darkness as Nick held me and prayed, then gently encouraged me to begin speaking Scripture over myself, his arms around me as the verses spilled out of my mouth:

"For God has not given us a spirit of fear and timidity, but of power, love and a sound mind ... Peace I bequeath you ... My peace I leave to you ... The fruit of the Spirit is ... Peace ... Then the peace of God which transcends all understanding will guard your heart and your mind."

Seconds, minutes, hours passed until eventually my heart began to slow to its normal pace and I fell asleep in Nick's arms.

* * *

About a month earlier we were on holiday with Nick's family in St Ives, Cornwall. Stuck in our B&B due to bad weather, I pressed my nose against the window as the rain poured down in heavy grey sheets. Resigning myself to staying inside I picked up a book which I'd been meaning to read for weeks. Then, without warning, the words stopped making sense. I blinked hard, hoping my eyes would come in to focus. They wouldn't. Each time I tried to read a line, my brain felt like it was going to explode. I started to panic.

"I'm going to lose everything in my mind," I thought. "I'm going to end up being taken away by men in white coats."

With each thought the walls in the room constricted. I couldn't breathe. I needed to get out into the fresh air.

I walked along the corridor to find Nick watching a movie with his brother and asked if he could come for a walk with me. "But it's raining?" he questioned. Yet something in my eyes told him that this was serious. We began to walk in the rain, hoods up, coats buttoned. Up, up, up a cliffside path until we were out into the air on the craggy, raw Cornish coastline. We leant over the railings, looking down at the curve of the shore. I began to drink in the space around me. The stormy waves crashed against the cliffs and sheets of rain kept blowing into us. We were getting drenched, but at least the walls weren't closing in on me any more.

"What's going on?" I could see the concern in Nick's eyes as I looked out over the cliffs, gulping in the salty air.

I opened my mouth to try and tell him what had happened, but my brain went blank. Where were the words? With another deep breath I tried again to make sense, but a whole sentence just didn't seem within my reach. "I, can't, don't … I feel, no…"

I couldn't articulate what was happening to me. I couldn't string the sentences together to explain coherently what was going on. He was evidently worried for me and frustrated that he couldn't understand what was happening, so Nick just held my hand, seeming to accept that his wife, who he usually couldn't stop talking was, for now, muted. He called to tell his family that we would not be joining them for dinner and we kept on walking. We walked and walked and walked. Eventually I was able to tell Nick what had happened in our room. We ended up in an empty restaurant where we ate quietly and took in the breathtaking beach view.

We drove back to Liverpool at the end of our holiday, dropping in on some close friends before heading home. Nick and I both thought it might help me to see some friends. As we ate together, I desperately wanted things to go back to normal. I was beginning to feel a little more like myself when the conversation turned to Pure and they began to ask me about what was happening.

Slowly I felt my mind close over again. I couldn't answer their questions. I couldn't even continue down one train of thought. I forced myself to stay at the table, but inside I just wanted to run away.

Following discussions with Nick and my mentor at the time I decided to take the next few days off work and leave the team to run the days in schools without me. For the first time in five years, I would not attend a school performance.

For the next days and weeks I struggled to be around people. Conversation and busy atmospheres were just too much for me. It felt like my ability to process information had suddenly been sucked away and there was nothing left. I would regularly find my mind suddenly just going blank, leaving me desperately grasping in the darkness for any wisp of a thought left in my mind. Little by little the words came back and I began to go back to work. My mind was still fragile and I was nervous about pushing it too far.

* * *

That night as I listened to my racing heartbeat in the dark, I knew something needed to change. The next day I went to see my doctor and was referred straight to a cardiologist for tests.

Pure had been gathering momentum during the past 12 months and I was working harder and harder to try and keep up with all the opportunities that were presenting themselves. By this time there were 12 people volunteering with me and I wrongly felt that I needed to work harder than any of them to validate their time. This was screwed up thinking and because of it I had pushed myself so hard that my body couldn't take it any more. Now, I was on the edge of burn out.

A few months before our holiday in St Ives, God had shown me a picture of a cruise ship where I was working hard in every room. Cooking in the kitchen, entertaining on stage, making up the beds and cleaning on deck. Gently He showed me that He didn't want me to be in all those rooms. I needed to be at the helm, so I could see where the ship was going. At the helm I would have a different perspective. I would be able to hear from God and direct the ship forward.

Through this picture God showed me that I was in all the rooms of Pure, teaching singing classes at our Creative Arts School, mentoring most of the team, acting in all our productions, writing and singing the songs we used, organising the bookings and much more. For Pure to grow I needed to step out of these rooms and up to the helm. I needed to change my thinking because God loved me too much to see me lose my mind over Pure.

God loves us far more than anything we could ever try and do for Him. He is much more concerned about our wholeness than our involvement in any project we are working on.

When money is tight and the workers are few, it is easy to try and fill every gap, because you think you can. But this only leads to burn out. I learnt this lesson the hard way. I was passionate about caring for the team around me, but I was setting an example that they couldn't follow without overworking themselves.

This really hit home when I noticed one of the team adopting a similar work pattern to me. I began to see that if I was leading the team, my behaviour set a precedent for everyone else to follow. The last thing I wanted to be building through Pure was the legacy of an overworked team. My actions had to change and if I was going to succeed in that I needed to change my thinking first.

30

DEALING WITH BURN OUT

When you're finally doing what you've dreamed of, when all you've hoped for is happening right before your eyes and you're playing your part in something so exciting that you can hardly believe it's real, it's very hard to stop. You want to keep going just in case you miss something. But if you don't look after yourself, you'll miss out on so much more.

Taking our place is not about soaring to superhero heights and neglecting our families, our relationships and ourselves. To take our place we need to have common sense and ensure we have our priorities in order.

If we haven't built good foundations when the things we've dreamed of finally begin to happen, problems can arise. If our character isn't based on God's truth, then it's very easy to start believing that we are the reason that all this is happening and that God depends on us for His work to continue. This couldn't be further from the truth and if we slip into this kind of thinking we're in dangerous territory.

Instead, I love how Deuteronomy 10:20 NLT puts it: *"You must fear the Lord your God and worship Him and cling to Him."*

Without realising it, I had subtly embraced the thinking that I was central to all the exciting things that were happening through Pure and that God needed me to work harder for it to continue. I made the mistake of starting to think I was a little bit super human. My schedule was jam packed. I woke up very early each morning, and worked late every night. My evenings were packed with mentoring different women. Until I came to the edge of burn out.

There are crucial lessons here that I had to learn – and if we learn such lessons, God will be able to use us more because we will have wisdom to handle the situations we find ourselves in.

When I started reading the stories of men and women whom God used powerfully in the 18th and 19th centuries, I discovered that this issue of burn out was not unique to me. Instead, it was an age-old problem that has incapacitated many people who God worked through in the past. Every single one of them started their journey with a zeal for God and the work He had given them to do, yet each of them at times failed to take care of themselves or their family.

Take Jennie Lake for example. God was using her husband mightily to heal many people. Word about what God was doing through him spread until there would regularly be people lining up outside their home each day, each one hoping that he might pray for them to be healed. Jennie spent all her time looking after those people while they waited for John to come home, so that she neglected herself until she got extremely ill and died prematurely. Many people say it was the exhaustion that killed her. If she had looked after herself, she may have lived longer.

"One point often ignored in ministry is that there will always be a 'need' to be fulfilled. One ministry can't meet all the needs that will appear, no matter how powerful and anointed that ministry seems to be. So common sense is invaluable to Christian ministry. The natural body and the natural family need attention, and the natural family should always be the core of any ministry." (Gods Generals, Roberts Liardon)

Each of us must learn to look after our own bodies and families before bowing to any external pressure to do more than we can physically do.

Another illustration of the importance of this is the life of Evan Roberts, the Welsh Revivalist. Evan was so passionate about seeing people meet with God that once God's presence began to outpour in Wales, he would stay and run revival meetings all through the night. He didn't rest or sleep, to the point where he had an emotional breakdown. When this happened, instead of taking some time out to rest and recuperate he was swayed by the criticism and demand of the people for him to continue. So he carried on these meetings until eventually he burnt out so badly that he stopped preaching.

As the work of Pure grew I had failed to take care of myself. I was carrying the burden of the ministry on my own shoulders, and now I was on the edge of burn out. Around this time I remember leading worship at a youth event. We were singing a song I'd written:

"When my heart is racing and the tears fall,
When my mind is failing and I can't see,
I know I can count on you...
So be my strength, be my strength, be my strength
Lift my head, lift my head, lift my head."

As we sang this song, I knew it applied to me more than ever. I didn't know how to change the way I felt, only God could be my strength. More than ever, I needed Him to lift my head and to shift my perspective so that I didn't burn out completely.

A month later, on the day Nick and I were about to fly to the US to attend a church conference in Baton Rouge, Louisiana, we discovered I was pregnant. Now more than ever I knew things needed to change.

One night at the conference a well known American evangelist with a healing ministry was speaking. The presence of God was heavy and thick in the room and as the speaker stood on the stage he listed different ailments that he felt God wanted to heal. One of these was arrhythmia, which is what I had been diagnosed with. I was too scared to go forward so instead from where I stood, I lifted my hands and said to God, "I know you can heal me here, right now. I know you can heal my heart."

Right then I felt something like electricity swarm through my body. Since then every test that has been done on my heart has been clear. I was completely healed.

When I returned from the US I began to step back from some of the roles I had been doing in Pure and was amazed how God had placed the right people within Pure to fill those gaps. My behaviour didn't change overnight, but as I prayed with friends and daily asked God for help, I began to find a different approach in my work. I realised that I had a limited amount of time and a limited amount of strength and that was okay. Every day I needed to do what I could and then entrust the rest to God.

Now I'm used to it. There is always more work to do than I have time for. But instead of overworking myself, I start the day by asking God to help me to do what He needs me to do. When the work mounts up and it's more than I can manage, I have learnt that I don't need to have everything perfectly boxed off. Instead of being frustrated, I need to learn to be content with what I can do.

"I am not saying this because I am in need, for I have learned to be content whatever the circumstances. I know what it is to be in need, and I know what it is to have plenty. I have learned the secret of being content in any and every situation, whether well fed or hungry, whether living in plenty or in want. I can do all this through him who gives me strength." (Philippians 4:11-13 NIV)

Time and time again I'm reminded that it's not about me and the work I can do. It is all about Him. We are his hands and feet, and He calls us to look after the bodies He has given us. When He can trust us with this, then what we are called to do can really flourish.

31

DISAPPOINTMENT

It was early October and I was in the car with one of our managers. We were chatting about what he was up to and how he was doing when, completely out of the blue, he began to tell me that he thought he had made a mistake by joining Pure and wanted to leave. Jack had left London to join our team six months prior to this. It had taken a long time for him to reach the decision to move. We had prayed about it together and God had confirmed it to him in several ways. There was no doubt in my mind about whether he was in the right place. But now these words had spilled out of his mouth:

"I've made a mistake, I need to go back to my job at Beech Ridge. That's where I'm meant to be."

He had left his job as a primary school teacher at Beech Ridge to join Pure only half a year ago. I couldn't understand it.

The team at Pure had been growing rapidly at this time. People were coming from across the country to join us and with more people on board we were able to do more than we had ever done before. New, exciting partnerships were emerging with key organisations and new performances and programmes were being developed. Then, just as we were developing our first ever tour and about to market our first intern programme, I found myself having this conversation.

Disappointment doesn't even come close to describing how I felt. I was heartbroken. Jack was an exceptional manager and was doing a wonderful job. He was extremely creative, the team loved him, and he had an amazing ability to draw the best out of others. Together we had just created the best production to date in Pure's portfolio. I didn't want him to leave. Disappointment and confusion filled my heart. Had I made a mistake? Had I heard God wrong? All I could do was trust God and let Jack make his own decision. We said goodbye about six months later and as I prayed for his replacement God kept reminding me of this verse:

"But seek first the Kingdom of God, and His righteousness and all these things will be added to you." (Matthew 6:33 ESV)

This was the promise. I needed to seek God's Kingdom and His righteousness above anything else and trust that He would provide the rest.

As I went over the situation in my mind, I realised that I had pushed forward with what I thought was the best plan, instead of obeying God in the details. I couldn't help but wonder if Jack would have stayed if I had done things differently.

But there came a point when I just had to let it go, stop going over and over in my mind any mistakes I had made and move on. There comes a point where dwelling on yesterday's disappointment stops us from stepping into today's opportunities. I had to trust God and seek His Kingdom first.

We all face disappointment in our lives. It's how we deal with it that's important. We won't always understand why God lets things happen the way they do. Sometimes we have to lay down our right to understand and seek God amidst the pain and confusion.

When our first group of interns arrived I was excited about the year they were about to embark on, hoping it would be a challenging but encouraging time for them. Many doors had opened for us and there was so much opportunity from this new partnership. But then plans changed and our tour was delayed. Nothing was going quite as I'd hoped it would and I was reminded of my own gap year with Activate.

One of my hopes when I started my gap year was that I would

have really good pastoral support and be able to grow while I was on team. But I found this hard. I didn't get the support I was hoping for and it wasn't just me who was struggling. Midway through my year with Activate, tensions reached breaking point:

"I hate you, I wish you would leave, you make everything awful..."

Everywhere around me the team were raging, beating mats with their fists, shouting into space. This environment was the last place I wanted to be in and I was a little unsure how to handle what was going on. I felt bad for our leader who was trying his best. It certainly felt like things had gotten out of control.

We were in Wembley, London, for a week, working in schools in the area when Greg, our leader at that time, decided to lead the team in a drama exercise, where we took our emotions out on gym mats placed around the room. He obviously sensed that the tension in the team was rising. He must have thought that it would be good to let people vent and get it out. But instead we found ourselves in this horrendous situation. In the end, Greg's line manager was called in and led our team for the rest of the year.

We went through some really tough times that year – times where I questioned why and whether I was in the right place. I could have finished that year a little disappointed that it was not what I had hoped. Instead, I let each and every hard time drive me into God, asking Him what His purpose was in the pain, what He wanted to bring out of the mess and uncertainty.

Now I know that God used all those things that went wrong to teach me and grow my character. We have a choice in every situation to look for the hand of God at work and understand that within our struggles He has a greater plan, or to give in to disappointment. Dealing with disappointment isn't easy. But as we're honest with God, and lay down our hurt, He can heal us. There won't always be someone to take you by the hand and encourage you to turn to God. There will be times when you have to make the choice to go to God on your own when you're hurt or disappointed.

As I took my questions to God and handed over all my own expectations of what my gap year would be like, I was able to grow and learn from the experience. Instead of giving up, I became more flexible and open to God doing something different.

The way we deal with disappointment and knock-backs is crucial to how we become the people God has made us to be. When our prayers haven't been answered the way we'd hoped and things happen that we don't understand, we each have a choice to make. Will we step away from God and begin to blame Him or others for what has happened? Or will we go to Him with our broken hearts, our questions, and ask Him to show us the way ahead?

"I don't think we can fully step into our destiny until we have learned how to do two things: 1. Minister to ourselves. 2. Know how to navigate disappointment." (Bill Johnson)

Ministering to ourselves simply means learning how to care for ourselves. To be able to make space in our lives to hear from God and process the pain of disappointment until it's dealt with. Part of navigating times of disappointment is having people around us, who fly in formation with us and are able to challenge us and ask the tough questions. People who won't just agree with us, but will see the bigger picture and the areas where we need to grow.

In this life we're sure to encounter disappointment at some stage. What really matters is how we deal with it when it comes. Disappointment can either leave us bitter and twisted or wiser and more in tune with God. And it's our decision. Which will it be?

32

DEALING WITH DISAPPOINTMENT

Disappointment sits like a heavy weight that has built up over time. You can push it down or shrug it off, but unless you deal with it, a deep descending gloom is cast that infects all you do.

I stood rooted to the spot reading an email that had just come through. My heart began to pound as I realised the weight of the words I was reading. The email was from a partner organisation, regarding a project that they had promised to fund. Some of the team had been working on this particular project for the past few months and now it looked like it was no longer able to go ahead.

My heart sank as I thought about the impact this would have on our interns and the rest of performance team. How could I tell them that it was over, that all their hard work was for nothing?

I felt sick with frustration and hurt. I didn't want to tell anyone what had happened. That night I cried with disappointment, partly because I hated to think how the team would be impacted by the news, and partly because I was frustrated that my trust had been broken like this. I understood some of it was out of their hands, but I did truly believe God was going to use this work that we were partnering on.

For one night I let the disappointment hang over me. I rehearsed all the conversations that I had with this partner through the gloomy filter of what had happened. I knew I couldn't stay in this place.

The next morning, I got up, spent time with God and began to seek Him about this situation. As I prayed, I felt that we weren't to give up on this. God would make a way where there was no way. I went into the office and as we gathered as a team, I explained the situation and asked them to pray with me in line with what I felt God had been saying.

As we prayed together and declared this promise as a team, faith began to rise in us. We prayed for a turnaround, speaking out all the things we felt God wanted to do through this partnership and declared that a lack of finances could not stand in the way of what God wanted do. He was able to give us all the resources we needed.

After we prayed I felt it was right to reply to the email I had received and tell them what I felt God wanted to do through the project we were working on together. Later that day they responded by saying that in light of the email they had changed their minds. They would find the funds and move ahead with the project after all. It was such an encouragement to us, but it wasn't quite the end of the story. Though it did go ahead, the tour we had planned together was later delayed by a few months, which had a huge impact on the staff team and performance interns that we had specifically brought on for this project.

Hannah was one of those performance interns. She had been the first to sign up to our internship and was full of excitement when the year began. I had high hopes too. Then, when things out of my control meant that our tour was delayed, my hopes of providing the best internship ever were dashed and Hannah was left with a year that she had not signed up for:

"When I signed up to do an internship with Pure Creative Arts, I think it is safe to say that I expected my year to be plain sailing. I had watched other friends do various Christian gap years and since theirs had seemed to go according to plan, surely mine would too. I had images of me flying through the year and coming out the other side some sort of 'super Christian' (whatever that means).

As the year began things didn't quite go according to plan. I hit financial problems and the tour that I was supposed to go on didn't materialise as hoped. There were times when I was sitting in the office not quite knowing what I was meant to be doing there. And as my hopes of a plain sailing year seemed to crumble around me, so did my hope of becoming a 'super Christian'. Frustrated, I cried out to God. 'Lord this wasn't the plan ... why can't it be easier?... I thought you told me you wanted me here?'

But here in this time of frustration God began to do an amazing work in me, something I would never had expected in a million years. He taught me to trust in Him instead of trying to figure it all out by myself. In the 22 years of my Christian life, that's never been something that has come naturally to me.

I'm a planner. I like to know where I am going, what is next on the agenda. Lists, timetables, diaries excite me. I guess there is nothing wrong with this, in theory. It's good to be organised and have structure in your life. But for me it meant that when things didn't go the way they were planned, I got really stressed. When the future seemed uncertain, I worried. When I didn't quite know what was in store, I got anxious. And this anxiety churned within me, eating away at me from the inside. Instead of talking to God about my fears and concerns, I would think about them over and over, worrying until I became physically ill.

This is what began to happen at the start of this year and as I sat with this fear eating away at me, not quite sure where to go next, I was encouraged to give my fears and disappointments over to God. When I finally did, He began to speak to me about my perspective.

One week, while I was performing at a Christian conference, God showed me a picture of what my life looked like to Him. He saw me looking at my life through a telescope, focusing on all that wasn't working how I thought it would. Then other people walked up and placed their telescopes in front of mine, trying to get me to see my life through their perspective. But what God was telling me to do was to step back from the telescopes and look left to right, up and down. That huge wide perspective was how God saw my life. I had been so busy looking through my own telescope of life that I had forgotten that God had ultimate control – and He saw my future, my past and my present in a far bigger picture than my human head could ever comprehend.

As God began to change my perspective on life, gradually my attitude began to change too. I began to understand that God was far more interested in the state of my heart than the list of things I wanted to achieve in my life: a great husband, my own house, kids, a dream job, travelling the world. They were all good things to desire, but God's top priority for my life was shaping my heart to be more like His. I realised that my relationship with God and the openness of my heart to hearing Him was far more important than whether my 'five year plan' was working out.

I am supposed to start my teacher training course in September, but the funding has been cut and I don't know if I can afford to do it this year. A year ago this would have felt like the end of the world, a disaster of epic proportions. But now, it's okay. Whether I start my training this year or next, I know God has a plan. I know that God is calling me to be a teacher. How that happens and when it happens is currently beyond my control. But I trust that my Maker has it in hand.

If this internship with Pure had been plain sailing, I'm not sure I would have learnt so many valuable life lessons. I'm not sure I would have the same relationship I have with Jesus now – one that is far more based on love and trust than it has ever been. If I hadn't had to sit through the storms of life and wait in frustration, I wouldn't have been able to put into perspective

what is important in life – that God cares far more about my character and the state of my heart; that He is more concerned about being in relationship with me than what my next plan is. That knowledge has freed me up far more than I have ever felt in my life.

My finances are still a mess and I'm not really sure what I am going to be doing during the next three months. I'm certainly not a 'super Christian', but instead I'm His work in progress and I have the unconditional love of the Father. This in turn frees me up to 'act justly and to love mercy and to walk humbly' (Micah 6:8) and to continue learning. Which is far more important than anything else I could achieve in life. – Hannah. (PCA Intern 2012-13)

I was really disheartened when the tour that Hannah was expecting to perform in did not materialise as I had been promised it would. We had been let down by something beyond my control and I hated that I couldn't fix it. In all of this I realised again that I am not in control of whether someone has a good gap year or whether a tour happens or not. God is the only one who decides what will or won't happen and through it all I had to trust that He was working out His bigger and better plan.

Although the internship hadn't turned out how we had expected it to, God did something far more wonderful in Hannah that year than any tour could have achieved. I realised that perhaps my desire to run the perfect internship was, ultimately, more about me wanting people to have a great experience with Pure, than seeking God's best for the people who had signed up.

Dealing with our disappointments is only the first step. We need to learn from them too. If we don't learn from our mistakes, we'll just go round and round in circles. Next time someone approaches me about planning a tour together, I'll do a lot of things differently. Looking back, I can see the mistakes I made and I don't want to repeat them.

One big thing I learnt is to hold exciting opportunities like this with open hands; lay them before God and trust that if they are from Him, He will make a way. We can't pin our hope on being encouraged by exciting opportunities or by people coming through for us. Our hope must always be in God. He's the one who opens the door, no one else. When we do this, we become more open to God changing the plan or doing things differently to how we expect. I am realising that His plans are much bigger than anything I can see or conceive, and when I let go or hold lightly what He has given or opened up, there is space for Him to do something greater.

Things will not always work out as we hope they will. Learning how to deal with disappointments along the way is essential when we're following God. If we don't deal with disappointment, it can become like a dirty, gloomy lens which taints everything we look at. Ultimately, we can either use disappointment to make us stronger or we can let it crush us. If we're going to take our place, to be all that He has called us to be, we need to get used to shrugging off disappointment and letting the experience fuel us further for the journey ahead.

33

RHYTHM

"Are you tired? Worn out? Burned out on religion? Come to me. Get away with me and you'll recover your life. I'll show you how to take a real rest. Walk with me and work with me – watch how I do it. Learn the unforced rhythms of grace. I won't lay anything heavy or ill-fitting on you. Keep company with me and you'll learn to live freely and lightly." (Matthew 11:28-30 MSG)

We were in a time of prayer at one of our quarterly team days when one of our school mentors came to me and shared a picture of God and me dancing together that he felt God had shown him. He felt that God was saying He wanted me to be led by Him and dance to His rhythm in all I was doing.

As the day came to an end, the image stuck with me and I pondered what it could mean. I thought about all the times I had watched people dance together. How one dancer is led by the other, supported. They move together, completely in sync.

How could I do this with God? How could I make sure I was lockstep with Him in all I did? Because I knew that if I did this, I would learn the unforced rhythms of grace.

Around the same time, my pastor Nic Harding was challenging me about the way I managed my time. "Tamsin, you're constantly operating at 100% of your capacity," he said, during one of our mentoring sessions.

"Isn't that what we are supposed to do?" I thought to myself. "What is the point of only giving 90% when you could give 100%?" But he was right. Though I had learned to step back a little since I had come close to burn out two years ago, my schedule was still crammed full, with almost no margin for the unexpected.

A week earlier a girl from my team had been raped. She came into the office the morning after it had happened. Straight away I could see that something was wrong. I took her for a walk and she told me what had happened. The next few days were spent with her while she was interviewed and examined and she moved into our home so we could support her.

What had happened to her was unimaginably hard to process. She needed time to talk, to be hugged and to be loved. I desperately wanted to be there as much as possible to help her. But because my schedule was already so full, being available meant something else would have to slip.

Nic Harding knew how close I had come to burn out less than two years ago and as my mentor he desperately wanted me to learn from my mistakes. As we talked about what had happened, he pointed out that my relentlessly busy schedule was not the best way to live. I needed to make space for the unexpected to be accommodated.

As a teenager, I loved spending time with people. Much to the frustration of my friends, I would organise back to back coffee dates, trying to squeeze in as many people as I could in the time that I had. I soon found out that not all of my friends appreciated it that much. As it turns out, they didn't want to be slotted into my schedule.

I started doing a similar thing when I met up with the girls I mentored individually. In an effort to ensure they all got my attention I'd slot them into appointments back to back, which meant they often ended up waiting around until I was finished with someone else before they could see me. It wasn't really the best way to make them feel valued.

There was something about the way I managed my time which reflected my full-on nature, wanting to do as much as I could with all of me. But the more I thought and prayed about it, the more I realised that there was something else going on beneath the surface. God began to speak to me about why being busy had become a rhythm of life for me.

My Dad is a wonderful godly man who has always worked exceptionally hard to achieve all that he has done. My Dad's father struggled with debt and addiction. As a result my Dad was forced to leave school at 16 so that he could get a job to support his family. Determined to prove to his family that he was not going to end up like them, he attended night school to finish his education. While they spent the evenings drunk, he escaped to his room and worked so hard that he eventually gained a place at Oxford University.

Since then, my Dad has continued working really hard and today is a professor of computer science and lectures at different universities across the UK. I am insanely proud of my Dad, but as I began thinking about how I managed my own time and drive, I started to realise how his work ethic and drive has rubbed off on me.

My Dad had to provide for his family where his own father had not managed to. He couldn't trust his own Dad to provide for him, he had to make everything happen himself. Later on, when my Dad became a Christian, he struggled to accept that his heavenly Father was very different from his earthly father. How could he trust his heavenly Father, when his own dad had not proved trustworthy?

If we have an earthly father who we need to provide for, protect and even make excuses for, then it's easy to start thinking our heavenly Father is similar and needs the same allowances. Before long, we find ourselves working to protect or even provide for God. Somewhere along the line, I picked up this kind of thinking and I realised that I'd never be able to learn "the unforced rhythms of grace" if deep down inside I believed God needed my help.

God is our heavenly Father, He doesn't need anything. Instead, He calls us to trust Him, to lean into Him and to let Him provide for us, not the other way round. It's so liberating to hand over a complex problem to God and rest in the assurance that He is holding all things and will show us what to do at the right time.

In the gospels we never see Jesus rushing about, trying to schedule in as much as possible. Much to the frustration of His disciples, He often takes detours, changes the plan and arrives late. He is never too concerned about other people's schedules. Instead we see complete obedience to what God has told Him to do.

Jesus did not try to work it all out Himself or try to provide for God. He looked to His Father and worked with Him in all He did. And Jesus asks the same from us:

*"Take My yoke upon you and learn from Me, for I am gentle and humble in heart, and **you will find rest for your souls**. 'For My yoke is easy and My burden is light.'"* (Matthew 11:29-30 ESV)

A yoke is a piece of ploughing equipment, which joins one horse to another so that they pull the plough together. Taking his yoke means that we stay connected to Jesus, follow His way, and allow Him to share the load. If you're worried about sharing a job with Jesus, He says not to. His yoke easy, the burden is light.

I have a habit of thinking that somehow it all depends on me; on how hard I work, on how much I do. I start thinking that I've got to work at 100% capacity all of the time or somehow I will miss out. But it's not true. Nothing depends on me or how hard I work. Everything depends on Him. All He asks for is my obedience. To stop myself from thinking like this, I find it helpful to pause and ask God at the beginning of each day, "What do you want me to do today? What is on your agenda for today?" and then try to act in obedience to what He says. The only way to do this is to stay close to Him.

"Remain in me, as I also remain in you. No branch can bear fruit by itself; it must remain in the vine. Neither can you bear fruit unless you remain in me." (John 15:4 NIV)

To 'remain' – or 'abide', as other translations put it – means to dwell in Him. In this passage we see that our job is to stay close to Jesus, it's His job to grow the fruit. It's not about us working as hard as we can to make something happen, all we need to do is move to His rhythm. When I let go and let God take the lead, I see His preparation and provision in circumstances.

There are times I've forgotten this truth and failed to trust that God can make a way. Instead of waiting for His direction, I've gone full steam ahead with my own plan – which usually involves me working really hard to make something happen and it rarely gets me anywhere. But when I've let go and allowed myself to follow His lead and work to His rhythm, He has made the way.

I hate when things happen which just aren't fair and when they do I want to fight until the situation is rectified. But that's not always my job and when I take it on as my own, I just get exhausted carrying a load that was never meant for me.

I need to step out of the ring and let God do the fighting.

"Commit your way to the Lord, Trust also in Him, and He will do it. He will bring forth your righteousness as the light and your judgment as the noonday. Rest in the Lord and wait patiently for Him." (Psalm 37:5-7 NAS)

God is the one who fights for me when it seems like I'm under attack. He has promised to champion my cause. The best place for me to be is sheltered in Him as I rest in Him and wait for Him do the rest. It doesn't mean that it's not our job to speak up in situations which are unfair or seek justice for those who are weak. We can do that in His strength. But when we are tempted to go in and fight for ourselves, often we need to let it go and ask God to do this on our behalf.

Moses led the Israelites out of slavery and towards the land that God had promised them. But because they were never able to fully trust God and obey His word, they went round and round in circles. The writer of Hebrews in the New Testament says that because of their lack of obedience they were never able to enter the rest that God had for them.

The Israelites were notorious for grumbling. God would provide, time would pass, they would forget about what God had done for them, and then they'd grumble some more. When Moses disappeared for a few weeks, they quickly demanded another god to worship and made a new one. They were never able to fully trust that God would look after them. Instead, they kept returning to their old habits of grumbling and trying to provide for themselves.

How often do we go around in circles on issues and fail to enter the rhythm of life that God has created for us? In His rhythm we're able to take the collisions, crashes and disappointments in our stride. In His rhythm He shows us when to hold back and when to move forward.

If we are going to be able to take our place to do all God has for us, we need to let Him take the lead in the dance of our life that He has choreographed.

34

MORE THAN WE'D BARGAINED FOR

One life. One unique thread. The minutes, the hours, the days, the years. The hoping, the waiting. The sharp intakes of breath, the belly laughter. The touch of a hand, the ache of love lost.
One thread, wound with dreams and passion, weaving through this world.
But one thread, surrendered to HIM.
Wound with His dreams and His passion.
Collides, criss-crosses, overlaps with other threads.
Pulled together to form something breathtaking, astonishing, mind blowing.
Out of the failed attempts, the good intentions,
The try-agains, the tears and the victories
A tapestry emerges.
There is no longer just one thread, there is a Holy mystery.
It is a mirror and it reflects HIM.

On a cold Friday afternoon in February we piled into my car and drove down to a youth event in Worcester where we had been invited to perform our production "Hold me" and speak about sex and relationships. Travelling to other cities wasn't new for us, we had taken our productions to a number of different cities, but this time I was leaving my nine-month-old son at home for the first time and it was much harder to go.

Following the performance, I spoke about the importance of purity and tried to give some practical advice about how we can avoid sin by becoming aware of our weaknesses. After I spoke, we prayed for a few of the young people and made the journey home. Then a road closure meant we were stuck on the motorway for hours in the middle of the night. We didn't arrive back till the early hours of the morning.

We have a lot of fun in the work we do. I can still remember how we laughed deliriously in the early hours of that morning, enjoying each other's company even though we were exhausted. But there's a cost too. A cost of time, energy and personal vulnerability, especially when sharing about a topic like sexual purity. We wondered if all this travelling really had been worth it. In that moment, it was hard to see what impact an event like that actually has.

A couple of years later our team was invited back to the same church and school in Worcester. I spoke at the church service on Sunday and at the end of the meeting a girl came up to me in tears. She told me that she was at the event I had spoken at two years before. At the time, she was dating a guy who wasn't a Christian. He was putting a lot of pressure on her to sleep with him and on the day of that event, she had finally decided that she would. But that evening, as she watched our performance and heard me speak about purity, God had spoken to her. She decided to end the relationship with her boyfriend and made a decision to follow God with all that she had. She went on to tell me that she dreamt of one day joining the Pure team herself.

Two days, two years apart and two collisions with the same girl gave an insight into the wider picture weaving around us. We will never know the full impact of what God is doing through us until we go to be with Him, but moments when we get a glimpse like this one are so precious. For us, that night was fairly ordinary, more an act of obedience than anything else, but for this girl, that night was the beginning of something very significant.

More recently we received an email from a girl who had heard me speak at a church conference when she was 13. What I had said about Pure had really resonated with her. After the meeting she came up to speak to me and I had given her my card. Now in her late teens, this girl still remembered that night, and got in touch to arrange a meeting with us because she wanted to be a part of something similar to Pure.

Another thread weaved criss-crossing in time.

No matter what it is, the work that God calls us to is never just about us. In everything we do there is an opportunity to touch the lives of others. And as we're obedient to God, we can trust that He is working through us. Another email we received reflected this:

"I wanted to send a message to Tamsin regarding her seminar 'The Turnaround Anointing' at Soul Survivor this year. I just wanted to let you know what a difference it has made to me! God really spoke to me through your seminar and worked in me through the prayer I received afterwards. I now really know God has given me a job to do here, because He thinks I am the best person to be doing it. I know He is equipping me with all I need and He's given me such confidence in building relationships without feeling I have to be a different kind of person.

In the couple of days after your seminar at Soul Survivor I had various incidents where God used the girls in our youth group to challenge me to do things I would have found difficult before and I found myself doing them without thinking about it! I feel such a deep love for our youth that is way beyond what I felt before and I've been running some girls' sessions on self-esteem and relationships and God is really working in that.

I've also been thinking about the future. I have always felt that there was another role for me, possibly within youth work, but I've not had the confidence to explore it, thinking I wasn't really a youth worker type. But God has been speaking to me about little things I can build on now and to expect big things for the future! I am excited about it rather than feeling that I'm not good enough to do what I would love to do! Anyway, a BIG thank you, God has used you to change my life!"

I love hearing stories like this one, where you see God working through one person to go on and impact others.

We are all called to influence people, wherever we are, whatever we do. As we're open to hearing God's voice and obeying Him, He will bring people into our lives that He wants us to impact. But it goes bigger than that. Each person has a network and when we impact one person it ricochets to impact thousands of other lives. God is weaving something together that is much bigger than we could ever imagine and we will never see the full picture until we get to heaven.

I first met Elikem at a Pure fundraiser event we were running in the summer of 2010. A member of my team introduced us, excitedly whispering to me that he was interested in joining the team. Then about a month later, he started coming to our morning prayer meetings. After hearing him pray, he had my attention. I realised that here was a man who sought after God's heart. He soon joined our team and began volunteering at our Creative Arts School around work commitments. Then he decided to take a year out of medicine and do an internship with us.

This was the year I really got to know him. Like everyone, Elikem came with his own story of struggles and pain. He had lost his Dad as a teenager and as a result struggled to understand his identity without a father figure in his life. In his will, his father had left Elikem his hospital in Ghana to look after when he was old enough, but now that the time had come, everything in him wanted to run away from this responsibility. God used Elikem's time at Pure powerfully to heal his heart and remind him of the leadership call on his life. As God revealed himself to Elikem as a Father, Elikem began to look at ways that he could help boys in the education system who were also fatherless and struggling to understand who they were. We worked together to develop the work Pure could do with boys and I caught a glimpse of the amazing leader that Elikem was.

This man was like dynamite. Before I knew it he was running events across the city to encourage men to be fathers to a younger generation of boys. He had connected with key leaders across the UK, was asked to be on planning groups for national conferences, and had developed a course for boys called Courageous.

With a small team Elikem began to run this course in schools across the city and we realised what a powerful tool it could be.

Kian came to our mentoring course after being banned from design lessons for fighting in the workshop. He was really responsive to all of the group sessions and, in the one-to-one sessions, it became apparent that he had suffered bullying himself and had got involved in fighting to stick up for one of the few close friends he had.

He also opened up about feeling abandoned by his dad, who lived in the same town but only bothered to see him a few times a year. We talked about how his dad's actions said more about his dad than anything that was wrong with Kian and I encouraged him not to give up hope on that relationship, but not to let it define him negatively either.

After continued discussion, it became clear that he had a real skill for design and the way things were put together, so we worked on a plan to help him go back in to his favourite lesson with a new plan on how to deal with his emotions and friendships, especially as he had so much potential in that area. He left excited about a chance to show his teachers that he could improve.

Bill *was recommended to the mentoring programme because his school saw that he had potential but was struggling behaviourally. He clearly had a short attention span and was erratic in the group sessions, but became a lot more engaged during the one-to-ones.*

It turned out that though he had an amazing foster family, he was still dealing with the after effects of an abusive and reckless home environment that he and his sister had been taken out of.

His younger foster brother was also from a similarly abusive environment and had developed a stutter as a result. We worked on ways that Bill could be a role model and support to his younger brother, and defend him from other's insults without resorting to insults or violence himself.

We also talked through his desire to join the army and his struggles with ADHD, and I encouraged him in the progress he had made in recent years and all the courage he had shown through his life so far. He left eager to continue his progress and do well in the future.

*From the first session it was clear that **Ollie** was a natural leader. The other lads followed his example and tone for better or worse. He was obviously smart and articulate, but was fairly open about his rebellious streak within lessons and around school in general.*

During one-to-one sessions he spoke about how, since his parents separated, his life had become a little more split, with weekends at his dads. He still played for his football team and, despite many promises from his dad that he'd be at his Sunday morning games, every Saturday night's drinking so far had meant that promise had yet to be fulfilled. He didn't go into too much depth, but at 13 he had already picked up on his older brothers' interest in alcohol and weed, so we looked at some of

the reasons why they did this, as well as the health impacts on someone of that age.

We spoke about his relationship with his mum, how he could make her feel loved and valued and work with her in establishing his boundaries and showing responsibility, rather than continually ignoring her instructions as he saw how that hurt her.

We also looked at his future plans as he wanted to be an actor. We spoke about opportunities to get involved in local drama groups and how, whether he made it professionally as an actor or not, he could use that skill to teach and help others in the future.

Elikem is now married and has decided to return to Ghana and run his father's hospital. But it was such a privilege to have his path collide with mine for those three years. The boys' work that he spearheaded within Pure still continues and though he has moved on to new things, I know the effect of his impact will ripple on well into the future.

All through the Bible there are chapters devoted to genealogies. Name after name is listed through history and we can see the lines of legacy. Reading these names reminds us that we are part of a long legacy of people through history. We have a place to take now, a baton to take from those who have gone before us. A baton that we in turn need to entrust to others.

35

LEGACY

It was the first time I had mentored Jessica and she came through the door full of laughter. But soon as we began to chat it became clear that all was not as it seemed.

She had wanted to see me and as she began to speak, tears streaming down her cheeks, she told me the story of the previous weekend – a guy from work, a party, how she had stayed the night, how they had shared a bed. He had wanted to sleep with her. She hadn't wanted to, but he had put the pressure on and she felt bad. She was in bed with him, what else could she do?

Questions flooded my head. Was she OK? Was this rape? Had they used contraception?

The answer to this last question was no.

Had she done a pregnancy test, I asked? She shook her head. Up until now she had been in denial that the weekend had even happened. The possible consequences hadn't even occurred to her.

A few days later she took the test to discover she was pregnant. One night, one guy, some pressure to do something she didn't really want to, and now a whole new life was in the picture. At this stage only Jessica's housemate and I knew.

Over the next few weeks we talked, she cried, she pushed into God, she went to church, she cried some more. I was amazed by how well she took this news. Never once did she consider any other option but keeping this little one. Never once did she let go of God, she only pushed into Him harder.

We talked about her fears about what people would think and what people would say. She shared her deeper fear that this would stop her from being able to meet the man of her dreams and get married to him; that she felt like she was tarnished goods now.

Through each conversation, we talked about God's faithfulness and I reminded her, "I know God has the best for you, Jessica. He will turn this around, just you wait and see."

Jessica moved home to be with her parents. She had a beautiful little girl. It was hard managing sleepless nights and a baby all by herself, but through this time she had never felt God closer. It was like this was make or break for her. She clung onto God as hard as she could.

A few months after her daughter was born, Jessica came back to Liverpool. During this time she reconnected with one of her closest male friends from her time in Liverpool and quickly they fell in love.

"At the time, I was really surprised that no one judged me at all through the whole thing, which was what I was expecting. Through this time, God used Isaiah 44:22 to speak to me:

'I have swept away your offences like a cloud, your sins like the morning mist. Return to me, for I have redeemed you.'

The truth that Jesus gave himself up on the cross became real for me in a whole new way. God had everything planned out and I just trusted in Him. Through this time, God put the right people around me. It felt like God was in every aspect of every detail, even down to the fact that Tamsin and I were pregnant at the same time!" –Jessica.

Six years later they are married with another little one. Jessica trusted God despite the overwhelming situation she faced. She could have run away or let shame rob her future and cause her to run in the opposite direction, but instead she ran into God and He made a way for Her. I know her daughter's life would have been very different if she hadn't turned to God at this time and I have no doubt that the impact of Jessica's life will reach out far beyond her family.

When Joy lived with us, it seemed impossible that she'd ever be free from the darkness that surrounded her. There were times when I wondered if she'd even live long enough to find out. But over the years I've watched as God's love has broken through and set her free. Things which used to lead her down dark paths, like her writing, God has turned for good. What started as a dark journal is now a victorious, love-blazing book called *Broken By Beauty*.

Jesus' life shows us the importance of living not just for ourselves, but to serve others. Jesus invested His time into people and He instructed us to do the same. Changed lives go on to change lives. This is what our legacy is to be. It's not about what we can achieve, how much money we can earn, or any awards we might get. It's about people. I still remember the day Joy came to me with an idea to help those who struggled with self-harm and eating disorders. A twelve week course we now run called Pure Freedom and it's helped many people who, like Joy, were struggling with life controlling issues. One of these was Rachel.

When we first met Rachel she was struggling with severe anorexia. Over the seven years that we worked with her, there were times where she nearly died because her weight was so low and her heartbeat had completely slowed down. The idea that she could be free from this struggle looked impossible, but as a team we believed God was enough to bring victory in her life even through the darkest times and eventually she saw freedom! Now, Rachel works with young people in China.

"When I reached my teenage years I got to the point where I broke down emotionally. I was a mess. I went through depression,

which I had to be medically treated for. I also developed an eating disorder. I just couldn't accept anything about myself. I found Pure Freedom really interesting to do because it was so useful and I needed to have one-to-one support. It challenges me to see myself as God sees me. It has helped me to see that even with the flaws and imperfections, I'm accepted, loved and I'm valuable because I know what God has created me to be."
–Rachel.

When I was a teenager, my youth leader had a vision of an army of young people leading other young people. She really believed that God could do this and spent a lot of her time investing in me and others in our youth group. This picture has always stuck with me and, in a sense, this is what my vision for Pure is. To see a generation rising out of schools who know their unique identity and are released into their full potential. An army of young people, leading other young people to be who they were created to be.

And it is happening. God is raising up mighty warriors who have been changed by His love and are now investing in the lives of others. This is where multiplication happens and it's how we pass on what God is doing from one generation to another.

I love it when young people who we've met through different programmes at Pure decide to come and join our team. They were children when we first met them, but now as young adults they've chosen to invest back into young people themselves.

Pure was never just about me and my dreams. It's a family of people who encourage, release and choose to see the best in each other. Our time together is about seeing each person step up and be released into the plans God has for them. Many people have joined Pure with a dream brewing in their hearts. They started volunteering on a programme we run and then slowly God has shown how our dreams fit together. Elikem,

Becky and Joy all had a piece of the picture within them and Pure wouldn't be the same without their input and that of many others like them. Sometimes people serve on our team for a while before God moves them on to something completely different. One year, half of our interns were moving on to teacher training courses. As we were praying for them I suddenly saw how this was all part of God's bigger picture. It was sad to see them leave at the end of the year, but God was sending each one of them out into the schools as teachers, so that they could be an influence there.

Others members of our team have moved on to other organisations or felt called to other countries. It's always sad to see people leave Pure, but God is working in all of this. It's not about one individual, one person, one organisation. It's about Him weaving all of us together.

It is amazing when prayers are answered and we see the turnaround in people's lives, but when it seems our prayers are not answered and things haven't worked out how we hoped they would, it's not always easy to see the bigger plan that God is weaving around us. Hearing stories of other prayers that God has answered, when ours haven't been, can be disheartening.

But even in the most hopeless of situations, when there's blood on the floor and it looks like it's all over, there is still room for God to work. Sometimes it will happen quickly and sometimes we may not see any good until years to come. Whenever I've dared to speak out in faith that God can turn a situation around, fear rises up in my throat...

"What if I've got it wrong this time? What if it doesn't happen and someone gets hurt?"

Those thoughts are normal, but as I've prayed in faith time and time again I have seen the faithfulness of God in unexpected and undeserved ways.

"The thought of my suffering and homelessness is bitter beyond words. I will never forget this awful time, as I grieve over my loss. Yet I still dare to hope when I remember this: The faithful love of the Lord never ends! His mercies never cease. Great is his faithfulness; his mercies begin afresh each morning.   I   say to myself, 'The Lord is my inheritance; therefore, I will hope in him!' The Lord is good to those who depend on him, to those who search for him. So it is good to wait quietly for salvation from the Lord." (Lamentations 3:19-26 NLT)

In each painful situation we have the opportunity to dare to hope; to remember how faithful God's love is; that He is our inheritance, the one we can trust.

Together, with God we are stronger. We all need to keep learning, keep growing and investing in those around us. It is not about what we can do as individuals, it is about each of us working together, playing our part to see God's plans happen on earth.

"So we keep on praying for you, asking our God to enable you to live a life worthy of His call. May He give you the power to accomplish all the good things your faith prompts you to do. Then the name of our Lord Jesus will be honoured because of the way you live, and you will be honoured along with Him. This is all made possible because of the grace of our God and Lord, Jesus Christ." (2 Thessalonians 11-12 NLT)

This is my prayer for each of you. That He would give you outrageous courage, that you'd know His power so that you can accomplish all the good things your faith prompts you to do.

If each of us did this, just think what kind of global legacy we'd see across our world in years to come.

36

IT'S ALL ABOUT HIM

You see an earthquake, I see an opening
You see a car wreck, I see you hope again
You see a dead end, I see you breaking through
You seem worn out, I'm making all things new

You see lost cause, I see a turn around,
You see unwanted, I see you finally found
You see a locked cage, I see an open door
You see dry bones, I see fire in your soul.

(Lyrics by Christina Boonstra, Tamsin Evans and Rael James)

"What you're doing with Pure is never going to succeed."

The words shot out of his mouth and dropped onto my chest like a ton of bricks. Here was someone I had known for years. Was is it true? Was everything I had been working at for the past twelve years fundamentally wrong?

This conversation came in the middle of an extremely difficult time in my life where some of the people closest to me began to question the very core of Pure's existence. With each new wave of criticism, I would wrestle with the words that had been spoken, desperate to be certain that I was learning, hearing from God and growing through it all.

Criticism wasn't new to me. Since the start of Pure there have always been some people who have questioned aspects of our theology and criticised our methods. Every time this happened I'd go back to the people I trusted: my church leaders, trustees and mentors, talking with them about what had been said. Their reassurance would make me feel safe in the fact that my own "family" did not agree with the criticisms that had been thrown at me. It was much easier to shake criticism off when those in leadership over me were not worried by it.

Seeking the help and support of those in leadership and around you is important. It is crucial to have people who have your back in what you are doing and can challenge mistakes, attitudes and your behaviour. I am so thankful for those who through this time supported and encouraged me through it. But even so, the approval of people can't ever be the safety net I rely on. If I did that, I could easily slip back into thinking that their opinion of me is more important than what God thinks.

When I faced criticism from within my own church family, I was really challenged by it. It was a lonely time of uncertainty, sadness and pain. Some of the people I had relied on for approval and encouragement had stopped providing it and now I felt like I was stumbling through the darkness. All I could do was reach out for Jesus and ask Him to navigate me through. I am thankful for those whom God put around me at that time from different places and churches who were able to encourage me and help me get perspective. Through this I realise that God was using this experience to ensure that I was not motivated by man's approval, only His.

"Even when I walk through the darkest valley, I will not be afraid, for you are close beside me." (Psalm 23:4 NIV)

The Bible never promises us an easy life. We are told that troubles will come our way and even our family may abandon us.

"Even if my father and mother abandon me, the Lord will hold me close." (Psalm 27:10 NLT)

Jesus was criticised, laughed at, accused of heresy and thrown out of cities, but it didn't put Him off. Even His closest friends deceived Him and still He completed what He set out to do. Through it all He shows love to each of them. Jesus made it quite clear that we should expect opposition too:

"Do you remember what I told you? 'A slave is not greater than the master.' Since they persecuted me, naturally they will persecute you. And if they had listened to me, they would listen to you." (John 15:12 NLT)

I am not sure why it came as such a shock to me that the people I loved would at some point criticise me, the Bible is so clear about it. When criticism comes, it doesn't mean it is time to give up. It's not even always a sign that we're doing something wrong. Sometimes, this kind of opposition is a sign that we're actually doing something right!

"Yes, and everyone who wants to live a godly life in Christ Jesus will suffer persecution." (2 Timothy 13:12 NLT)

In the West, very few of us know what persecution really looks like, but there are parts of the world where this is a daily reality. As I write, people in the Middle East are at risk of being beheaded unless they renounce their faith in Jesus Christ and in many other places Christians meet in secret for fear of their lives. We may not all face this kind of persecution, but we will probably all face some kind of opposition. When we do, we have to choose how we'll deal with it. Will we seek God, asking Him to teach us through it? Or will we let people's opinion define what we do?

In that dark time I had to make a choice about how I would respond. Would I see a dead end or would I see God breaking through? Daily I had to ask God to help me withstand this criticism with grace, choosing to love and forgive those who hurt me and being humble enough to learn along the way. Sometimes it's hard to see what God is doing when we face criticism or persecution. In this time we have to let go of trying to figure it all out and ask God to help us remember that nobody is perfect. People with good intentions will sometimes hurt us by accident. It's no use getting defensive or offended by them. The Bible tells us that our fight isn't with people. We have to look at the bigger picture and remember that ours is a spiritual battle:

"For we are not fighting against flesh-and-blood enemies, but against evil rulers and authorities of the unseen world, against mighty powers in this dark world, and against evil spirits in the heavenly places." (Ephesians 6:12 NLT)

When we remember this, we can look beyond the hurt and ask God to show us if, in fact, there is something else going on beneath the surface. This could be a spiritual attack set up to distract or confuse us. God has given us the power through prayer and His word to overcome opposition at times like this.

Often, it's less clear. Things aren't always black and white and we will never see the whole picture clearly. But one day all will become clear.

"We don't yet see things clearly. We're squinting in a fog, peering through a mist. But it won't be long before the weather clears and the sun shines bright! We'll see it all then, see it all as clearly as God sees us, knowing him directly just as he knows us!" (1 Corinthians 13:12 MSG)

Keeping these two truths in the forefront of our minds is really important when we're facing difficult situations. If we can do this, then we can face people who have hurt us with grace, always looking to find their good intentions beyond the hurtful words. We can be humble and not feel the need to fight or make our voice heard, remembering that it's not about us and what we achieve. It's not about proving that we're right, but instead doing what God has called us to do, in harmony with others.

One night during this time, when criticism seemed to be

coming at me from every angle, I woke up in the early hours of the morning and sensed God calling me to pray. I had a particular worship song in my head, a song which God had really used over the past five years to challenge me to pray into specific situations. Eventually I realised I needed to respond to this and went downstairs to the kitchen. Without thinking, I put my iPhone on shuffle, and immediately that same song started to play. God had my attention.

As I started to pray, I realised that through this difficult time I had become so fixated on the criticism that I was facing and the hurt I felt, that I had completely lost perspective on what was really important. I began to pour out my heart to God, talking to Him about everything that had happened. Slowly, I came to see that I needed to forgive the people who had hurt me and as I began to let go of the pain they had caused me, I was reminded again of the glorious wonder of the God who I'm living for.

I began to read the first few chapters of the book of Revelation in the New Testament and verses about God's greatness began to jump out at me. My focus was reset, my eyes fixed again on Him who is in control of everything, infinitely powerful and awe-strikingly beautiful.

Sometimes, in the difficult parts of the journey, we can forget why we started out in the first place. We get bogged down with trying to understand what is right and wrong and how to move forward. Our minds can become so consumed with problems that we forget to stop and focus on the wonder of Jesus. And here in my kitchen in the middle of the night, I was reminded all over again.

He is the one who begins all things, who with His words created the universe, and He is the only one who can resurrect what is dead and buried. Any man-made institution, organisation or business pales in comparison to the greatness of God and the words of critics are nothing compared to His words.

He never said it would be easy. In fact, He promised the very opposite. But in every moment we can be certain that He is with us. Whereever we go, whatever place God puts us in, whoever we are called to work with. Never let us forget that it is all about Him. Everything we do is for Him.

"You are worthy, O Lord our God, to receive glory and honour and power." (Revelation 4:10 NIV)

37

TAKE YOUR PLACE

"The world has yet to see what God can do with a person fully consecrated to Him, with Gods help, I aim to be that person."
– Henry Varley.

As I write this last chapter, Nick and I have just closed the front door to our former home in Liverpool and we are relocating to New York to continue following God's adventure for our lives. I am reminded once again of the words of Hebrews 11:8:

"It was by faith that Abraham obeyed when God called him to leave home and go to another land that God would give him as his inheritance. He went without knowing where he was going."
(NLT)

What does it mean to "take your place"? It is a call to the depths of your spirit; a call into the unknown; a wake-up call for you to seek the Lord and hear His answer.

What does that call mean for you?

Abraham is first mentioned in the Bible as "Abram" in Genesis 12 under a section titled "The call of Abram". He was called to leave all he knew that was comfortable to him and step into the unknown with only a promise of God's blessing. It is easy to read about what he did and not grasp the full weight of the risk he took, since we know the outcome already. Yet Abram consecrated his life to God and went, not knowing where he was going.

Taking your place is not meant to be easy. It is about obedience, about trusting God beyond that which you can see with your natural eyes. But it is the most exhilarating adventure you will ever have. The call to take *your* place and pursue God's dream for *your* life is not something I push out to you from the comfort of my own cozy life – I am keenly aware of what it means to live in the place where all one has to depend on is God. But you have to trust that He has a plan for you, even when you can't see or feel it. I pray that you do decide to trust Him wholeheartedly.

"Those who trust in the Lord will possess the land." (Psalm 37:9 NIV)

There is no one else who can do the things you were made to do. Therefore, this is not a time for you to shrink back, think small, give up or make excuses about why now isn't the right time. You need to get into God's presence and cling to Him. As you do, you will begin to see things as He sees them. Now is the time for you to be fully consecrated to Him. I promise you that there is a call on your life. It is tailor made for you. It is meant to scare you witless and challenge you, but simultaneously thrill you to the very core. It was what you were made for.

My heart is that as you come to the end of this book, you can use the following words to take hold of what that call looks like for you and to be brave and step out to take your place.

Challenge one: get into God's presence like never before and let Him show you who you are.

Challenge two: be only who He created you to be. Don't try to be anyone else. Don't waste your life trying to be or do anything that you were not made for. Instead, take time to consider what His call means for you.

"Almost every man wastes part of his life in attempts to display qualities which he does not possess ... and gain applause which he cannot keep." – Samuel Johnson.

Challenge three: "Take courage". In Joshua 1, Joshua is told over and over again to *"be strong and courageous"* as he is instructed by God to go and take new land.

We need to "take courage" to step out and take a risk. Stepping out and following God is never going to be easy, so don't be surprised when you come up against resistance. Resistance builds character. It helps shape us into the people we are meant to be. Learn to embrace it. Whether you are aware of it or not, God is alwasy present, cheering you on.

Never give up. Even when you think that you have messed up and God could never use you, He still declares that you are more than a conqueror in Christ.

"No despite all these things, overwhelming victory is ours through Christ, who loves us." (Romans 8:37 NLT)

"Despite all these things" means our mistakes, failures, life's situations... God has already dealt with them all. No matter how much you have messed up, keep going and rest in His grace. You can make a difference – more so, in fact, through your weakness. It is through your weakness that His strength is perfected.

It was never about you or me, it has always been about Him. He is the One who does it, who makes the way, who strengthens, equips, parts the seas and does the impossible.

You have a unique place to take – a place that connects and weaves together with countless others, as they also take their place. Now you have read this, you have a response to make. What will it be? Are you ready to fully trust Him? Are you ready for an adventure?

"Put your hope in the Lord. Travel steadily along his path. He will honour you by giving you the land." (Psalm 37:34)

ABOUT PURE

Pure Creative Arts is a dynamic charity using
theatre-in-education productions, interactive workshops
and ongoing mentoring projects in schools and
youth groups across Merseyside and beyond.
We tackle issues that young people often
find hardest to talk about.

For more information visit our website at:
www.purecreativearts.co.uk

Or call us on **0151 427 6777**